THE PATENT NARROW GA
OF
JOHN BARRACLOU

E.A. Wade

Narrow Gauge Railway Society

Special issue of THE NARROW GAUGE
No. 113   **Winter 1986/87**

JOHN BARRACLOUGH FELL

"MR. FELL'S PLAN IS ADMIRABLE"

John Barraclough Fell was perhaps the epitome of the self made Victorian man. He was born in London in 1815 but, when he was about twenty, he moved with his family to the Lake District; residing in Greenodd and Sparkbridge. It was from there, in the 1840s, that he carried out his first railway contracts in connection with the Furness and Whitehaven Railway. He went to Italy in 1852 where, as part of the firm of Brassey, Jackson, Fell and Joplin he was involved in the construction of several of the early Italian railways; including the Central of Italy, the Maremma and the Genoa and Voltre lines. On his frequent trips to Italy he was forced to cross the Mont Cenis pass by road, and it was this laborious journey that led him to turn his inventive mind to the problems of traction on mountain railways.

The result of his cogitations were two patents, taken out in 1863 (followed by a further three in 1866, 1869 and 1895 respectively) relating to the 'Centre-Rail System' for which he became justly famous. In this system the locomotives on mountain railways, engineered by Fell, were fitted with extra horizontal, powered wheels which could be made, when necessary, to grip a third rail (fitted between the two normal rails) and thus provide additional traction or braking power. Experiments were carried out in the years 1864/5 on the Gotland Incline of the Cromford and High Peak Railway in Derbyshire and the system was subsequently used on the Mont Cenis Railway, over the Alps, between St Michel in France and Susa in Italy. The line was opened in 1868 and had an eminently successful life until it was eventually replaced by a tunnel. The centre-rail system was later used for the Cantagallo Railway in Brazil and over the Rimutaka Incline in New Zealand from 1878, until it too was replaced by a tunnel in 1955. The invention was also utilized by Fell's son, George Noble Fell, on the Snaefell Mountain Railway in the Isle of Man; but here it was used only in a braking capacity. Although Fell's centre-rail lines were, strictly speaking, of narrow gauge (all having a gauge in excess of 3ft) they will not be discussed in the present work which relates solely to his non-centre-rail lines, all of which were of 3ft gauge or less.

It was the centre-rail system which made John Barraclough Fell famous but, although his most successful, it was by no means his only invention. In March 1868 he took out a patent for a form of steam powered monorail; the opening paragraph of which ran as follows: "For the purpose of obtaining greater economy, efficiency and safety in the construction, maintenance and working of railways and tramways than by the ordinary method, I propose to employ either a single rail in place of the two ordinary rails, or otherwise two rails of such a form and so connected together as to have the bearing properties of a girder or beam. I propose to combine this method of construction with the centre-rail system, as shewn in the Specifications of my Patents (of 1863 and 1866) with certain modifications in and additions to the manner of applying the guiding and gripping power of the wheels of the engines and carriages described therein". Thus, it will be appreciated that Fell's monorail proposals were a development of his earlier invention rather than a new departure. This process of development will be seen to run through all his later patents. It should also be noted that his 'monorail' patent allowed for the use of two bearing rails rather than one, if desirable. The monorail patent consisted of seven parts, the first and fourth of which related to the construction of the trackwork; "the rail being of a girder form so as to admit of the supports being placed at greater distances apart than is usual in ordinary railways, and of such shape as to allow guiding and gripping wheels to be worked either on the vertical web or on the upper or under flange of the rail. The supports may be constructed of wood, iron, brick or stone...so arranged as to dispense with a continuous formation of ballast, masonry or earthworks".

When two bearing rails were employed they were "tied together with plates or cross braces...(and) the gauge of these railways must necessarily be narrow, generally not exceeding two feet". The second part of the patent was for a steam locomotive designed for working on the single rail. It was to have two boilers (with marine fireboxes) hanging, pannier fashion, on either side of the carrying rail (thus putting the centre of gravity below rail level) with cylinders above or between the boilers. The loco was to be suspended from two double flanged vertical wheels and four horizontal guide wheels were to be fixed below the boilers (two on each side). These guide wheels would run against two further rails and would serve to steady the locomotive. They could also be powered by the locomotive and used to provide extra traction. Locomotives employed on the two carrying rail version of the system (the fifth part of the patent) "may be either like those already described, or having only one boiler placed above the rails with the cylinder and wheels beneath it, provided or not with guide and gripping wheels". The third and sixth parts of the patent deal with the types of carriages and wagons which would be employed on such lines and they follow the same principles as the locomotives. That is to say that they would be constructed in pannier fashion on the true monorail and, on the double rail

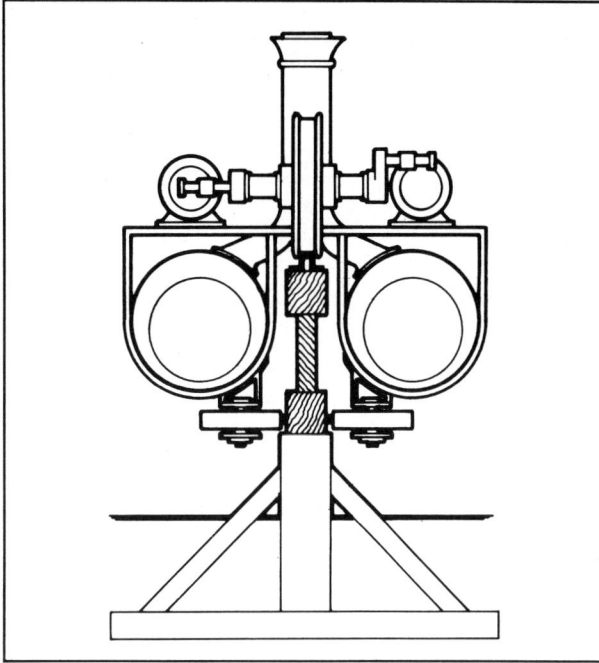

THE MONORAIL LOCOMOTIVE
from patent number 766 of 1868

system, they would be of pannier type, or completely above rail level if the gauge allowed. The seventh part of the patent consisted "of a contrivance for applying sand to the driving wheels of the engine, whether they be vertical or horizontal, also for cleaning the surfaces of those wheels and of the rails from ice, dirt and whatever may tend to lessen the adhesion". This involved the use of brushes, bearing against the wheel surfaces, being used to apply a fluid adhesive, on to which sand was subsequently thrown and made to adhere; and the use of rotating brushes to clean the rails. This was not really an important part of the patent as it could, as Fell admits, be used "not only in the engine included in this Specification, but also in any other engines where the above objects are desired to be effected". Fell considered that "A tramway of this description requiring no earthworks or masonry and occupying but little land may be constructed at a small expense, and as the frictional resistances are found to be less than on ordinary tramways the cost of traction is diminished. This description of tramway will be especially useful for mines and quarries, and

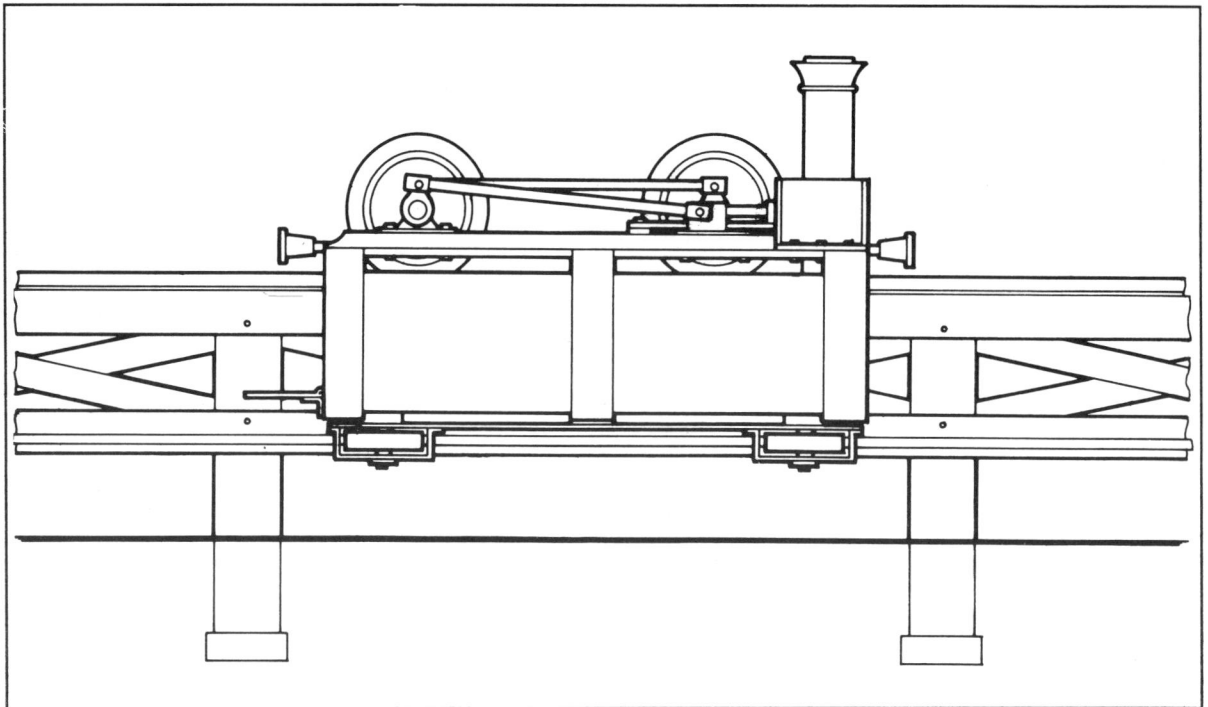

THE MONORAIL LOCOMOTIVE from patent number 766 of 1868

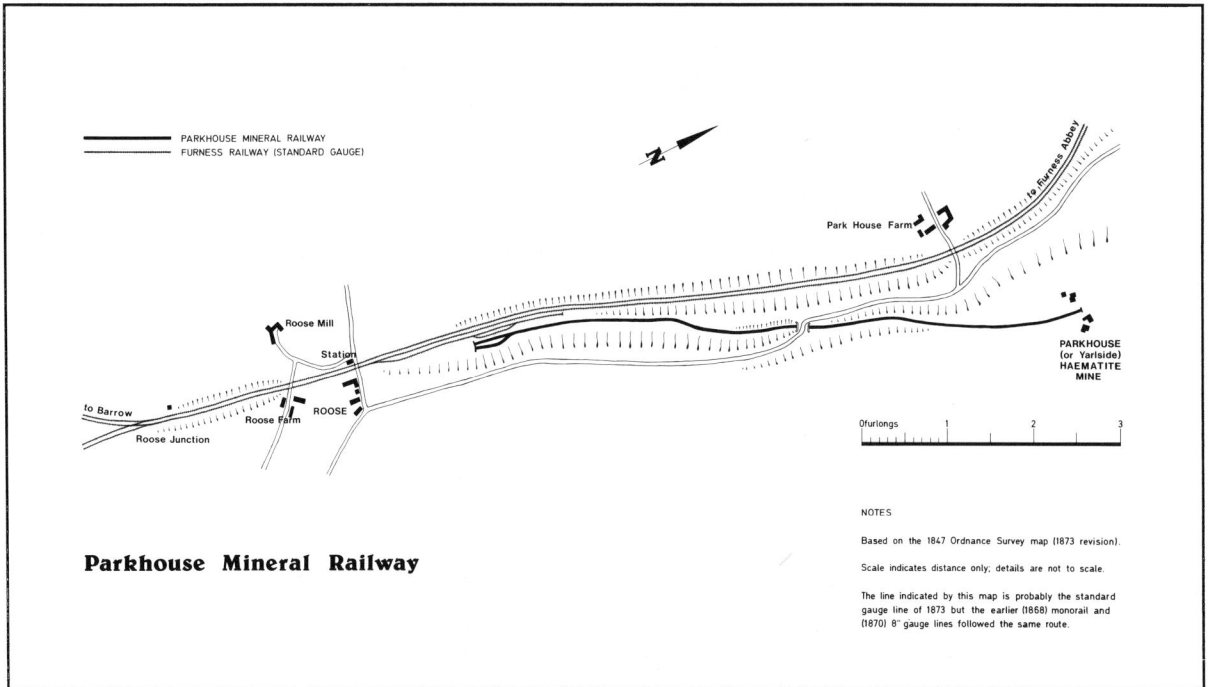

PARKHOUSE MINERAL RAILWAY
FURNESS RAILWAY (STANDARD GAUGE)

Parkhouse Mineral Railway

NOTES

Based on the 1847 Ordnance Survey map (1873 revision).

Scale indicates distance only; details are not to scale.

The line indicated by this map is probably the standard gauge line of 1873 but the earlier (1868) monorail and (1870) 8" gauge lines followed the same route.

wherever a cheaper method of construction than that now in use is required". Fell also visualised the use of hardwood running and guide rails and rubber tyred wheels as a means of increasing adhesion and reducing wear and tear, and the utilization of racks and toothed wheels for ascending steep inclines.

It would appear that only one Fell monorail was ever built, and it was something of a homecoming for him. It was constructed in 1868 to link the Parkhouse (or Yarlside) Haematite Mine and the Furness Railway near Barrow-in-Furness in, What was then, North Lancashire. The mines were operated by the Yarlside Mining Company, the principal directors of which were Messrs Boulton and Storey who, in earlier days, had traded as Boulton, Storey and Co. The firm was established circa 1856, became a subsidiary of the Barrow Haematite Steel Co Ltd in July 1892 and closed in 1902. The mines were later re-opened, only to close once more.

The Parkhouse Mineral Railway (as it was known) did away with the need for horse cartage and was a little over a mile in length. A Furness Railway minute of 27 February 1868 states, "works to proceed in connection with the new tramway to the mines of the Yarlside Company" and probably refers to the transfer siding constructed by the FR to serve the new line. The whole line was elevated above ground level and was fitted with guide rails. The steepest gradient on the line was 1 in 30 and the flattest about 1 in 48; the average being 1 in 35. It had curves of five to ten chains radius. The elevation of the railway varied from 3ft to 20ft and it passed over undulating country, fences, roads and streams without the construction of any earthworks or masonry. The wagons which ran on this line were constructed in pannier fashion and were fitted with guide wheels. They were designed to carry a load of some 5cwt of iron ore in each pannier and the resulting centre of gravity was about 9in below rail level.

It would seem that the carrying capacity of this monorail line proved insufficient for the railway was re-opened in January 1870, having been rebuilt with two rails laid to a gauge of 8in and provided with new wagons, of 4ft 6in x 2ft 3in internal dimensions. They could carry 1 ton of ore and were suspended from their axles (the wheels being at the ends of the wagons) by which means a reasonably low centre of gravity was still maintained; probably being at about axle level. The four horizontal guide wheels were retained of course, which ensured complete stability and made it impossible for the wagons to leave the rails. At first all wagons were fitted with the guide wheels, which had no flanges, but they were later used only on the first and last wagons on a train. It would appear that the original monorail line was horse worked for the *Barrow Herald* of November 1870 contained details of horses for sale, on account of the completion of Fell's new tramway. The

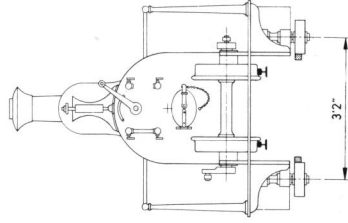

J.B.Fell 1871
Patent No.1

Cylinders - 5½"bore x 10"stroke
Wheel dia - 15"   Gauge - 1'6"
© E.A Wade 2/1985

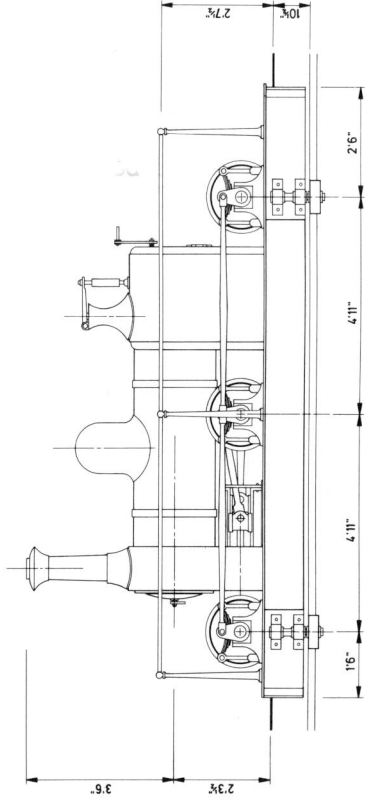

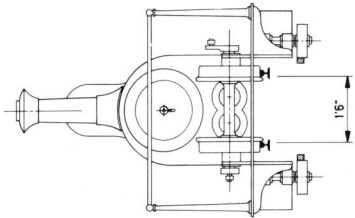

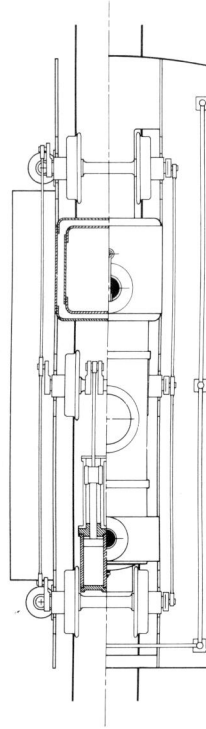

3'2"

2'7¼"

10¾"

2'6"

4'11"

4'11"

1'6"

3'6"

2'3¾"

1'6"

NOTES

Original patent drawing not
dimensioned. Gauge of 1'6" is
assumed.

Springs omitted from end
elevations and plan.

12" 6" 0feet   1   2   3

8in line may have utilised these horses initially but, after their departure, was worked instead by a stationary engine and an endless wire rope. This rope ran around a Fowler's clip drum at the engine end of the railway and an ordinary horizontal drum at the other. The rope was attached to the train by means of a clip on the side of the leading wagon, which held the rope tightly and could be easily released. The train could be reversed by attaching the clip on the other side of the train where, of course, the endless rope was running in the opposite direction. The trackwork consisted of two 9in x 3in planks, laid on edge at 9in centres, which were supported on trestles. The top of these planks were covered with short pieces of 1.1/2in thick timber laid crosswise and spiked down to them. On top of this, two 3in x 1.1/2in longitudinal sleepers were secured with a piece of felt being laid between the sleepers and the cross timbers to make up for any uneveness. The iron rails, which were simple 1.1/2in x 1/2in bar, were screwed down to the sleepers with a further piece of felt beneath them. The screwheads were countersunk into the rails. The guide rails consisted of 2.1/2in x 1.1/2in timbers, spiked to the sides of the 9in x 3in planks which formed the girder. The trestles which supported this structure were equally simple in construction but their precise details are now known. The railway, when built, was expected to carry a traffic of some 50,000 tons per annum (although it could accommodate about 100,000 tons) and it was constructed at a cost of £1,000 per mile; not including stations or rolling stock. The estimated saving in the cost of transport of the ore was 6d per ton per mile.

On 23 September 1870, Fell read a paper before the British Association, at Liverpool, on 'Central Rail Railways and the Advantages of Narrow Gauge Railways' from which we learn that..."In Switzerland, application has been made to the Government of the Canton Vaud for a passenger line on this principle, from the town of Lausanne to the Lake of Geneva. Plans have also been laid before the War Office for accelerating military transport in foreign countries and before the Governor-General of India for the construction of cheap branches from the trunk lines in that country. The gauge of these railways may be from 6in to 18in. They may be of wood or iron, or of the two combined, and may be worked by either stationary engines or by locomotives of a form specially designed for the purpose. They have the advantage of being economical in both construction and working, they occupy but little land and cause no severance, they may be erected with great rapidity and, being portable, may be removed when no longer required and re-erected in another locality. Before the war (the Franco- Prussian War of 1870/71) commenced an offer was made to the French Government to construct one of these portable railways to supply their army with from 1,000 to 3,000 tons of ammunition and provisions per day. The work would have been undertaken by a gentleman in Paris, who, with a force of 2,500 men, would have constructed from four to five miles of railway per day, following the advance of the army into Germany. The result has, however, shown how little such a provision was needed." The final sentence is an ironic reference to the fact that the French army collapsed in the face of the Prussian onslaught and Napoleon III surrendered, at the head of 80,000 men, after only six weeks.

Nothing appears to have come of the proposed railways in Switzerland or India, but the plans which Fell put before the War Office did bear fruit. A sub-committee of the Royal Engineers Committee was dispatched to Furness, where they visited the Parkhouse Mineral Railway, in company with John Barraclough Fell, on 6 September 1870. They noted that the wooden guide rails "show little sign of wheel marks and the horizontal wheels seem to do little or no work except at curves, and then come into play but slightly, which is the more remarkable as no cant is given to the rails". These unflanged horizontal wheels were, of course, only used as guide wheels. Fell's idea of using the horizontal wheels, as in his centre rail system, to supply additional traction, could not be realised at Parkhouse as the line was not locomotive worked. The system appears to have been even more stable than Fell envisaged and the guide wheels really only provided extra security against accident. As chance would have it, an accident occured whilst the sub-committee were inspecting the line. It was occasioned by the incorrect positioning of one of the drums around which the endless rope ran and, "The clip when released did not drop the rope, the drum pressing it against the clip, and the friction being sufficient to prevent its sliding, the train, instead of stopping, ran with considerable speed over the horizontal drum at the end of the line, lifting it and its trolly out of their place and upsetting them and nearly cutting the rope in two, yet although all this work was applied to one side only of the leading wagon it did not throw it off the rails". The sub-committee were clearly impressed with Fell's invention and admitted that the guide wheels gave the trains a stability far in excess of what could be expected from such a narrow gauge. They travelled on the line at various speeds and remarked on the smooth running of the wagons and their freedom from oscillation; although they were only built for mineral traffic. However, it was obvious that for such a railway to have a military application, it must be worked by a locomotive. Fell assured them that this was possible and that the gauge necessary for such a line would be from 15 to 18 inches.

The sub-committee subsequently reported back to the Royal Engineers Committee and made a number of recommendations. They felt that a prototype, locomotive worked railway should be constructed somewhere, with at least one locomotive and enough wagons to thoroughly test the system. They considered that such a railway could be laid both quickly and easily on service "and would have been invaluable in the Crimea or Abyssinia". It was appreciated that the trestles, in heights of 10, 20, 30 and 40ft , could be prefabricated in England and the railway erected in a narrow confined space without interfering with existing roads. The sub-committee felt that the wagons would need to be at least 7ft long and 6ft wide and that some should be equipped with springing sufficient to carry sick and wounded men. It was considered that the weight limit for a locomotive to work such a line would be 10 tons and that, if such a locomotive could be proved capable of the work required of it, the system would "prove most valuable for military purposes". The Committee noted "that Mr Fell proposes to use the horizontal wheels of his locomotive for gripping the side rails precisely, as in the Mont Cenis Railway the centre rail is gripped. For military purposes all carriages should be provided with at least two horizontal wheels with flanges, and a very light iron rail for them to run on". Fell had mentioned to a member of the sub-committee that he would be prepared to construct a line, one mile long, and supply ten wagons and a locomotive, capable of ascending gradients of 1 in 12, for the sum of £3,000. This was to be subject to any conditions that might be specified by the Royal Engineers Committee. It was considered that the heaviest loads to be carried would probably occupy two wagons, thus distributing the load, and that light but bulky loads, such as hay, tents and blankets, would present no problem. The advantages claimed by Fell for his railway system were summarised as follows: "It is cheap, portable, easily and quickly constructed. The locomotive has great tractive powers from the gripping of the horizontal wheels, thus enabling sharp gradients to be overcome. The weight of each part of the wagons and engine is small, thus enabling the whole to be handled without expensive plant. There is great freedom from oscillation and the narrowness of the gauge allows sharp curves to be passed without difficulty". On 11 November 1870, the Committee examined the plans of Fell's railway system and, following discussion, adopted the report of the sub-committee. The Secretary was directed to write to Fell, requesting a "detailed drawing and specification for a locomotive of 18in gauge capable of ascending gradients of 1 in 50, and the cost of such an engine from some maker of eminence".

In January 1871, Fell was granted his sixth patent which was for locomotives suitable for working a railway such as he was proposing to the War Office. In this patent Fell states, "My Invention relates to an improved form of locomotive engine for working on narrow gauge railways, being improvements upon those described in the Specification of my Patent, No 766, 'A.D. 1868' (the 'monorail' patent). The object of my Invention being to use only one boiler and yet bring down the centre of gravity of the engine lower than in those of ordinary construction, whereby greater steadiness and stability is obtained when running. Instead of using two boilers...only one boiler is placed above the carrying rails, but brought down nearly to their level by the leading wheels being placed in front of the smoke box, the trailing wheels behind the fire-box, and a third or more pairs of wheels when desired being placed under the barrel of the boiler. The side frames are of the usual form, but inverted, the horn plates projecting upwards, the principal part of the weight of the frames being near or below the level of the carrying rails. The water tanks (one on each side of the engine) are attached to the side frames; guide wheels on vertical axles are used to act upon the guide rails as an additional protection against getting off the rails, and also...to give increased steadiness and stability to the engine". Detailed plans and elevations of such a locomotive accompanied the patent and the side elevation appeared in two forms, with detail differences. The most significant of these differences is that, on one elevation, the guide wheels are shown to have flanges which were to run below the guide rails.* There is no mention in the patent of using these horizontal wheels to provide extra traction, and the drawings do not allow of such a use. However, the patent does state itself to be an improvement on the 'monorail' patent which did make such allowance. The patent drawing showed an engine with two inside cylinders but the patent also envisaged the use of outside cylinders; either above, at, or below rail level. It also allowed for the side tanks to be replaced by a tender and it will be noted that the patent drawing makes no provision for coal storage. In a review of this patent, the 8 December 1871 edition of the journal *Engineering* stated, "Whether it is worth while doing so much to gain so little, is a point regarding which we and Mr Fell hold very different opinions. As a scheme for necessitating the construction of an expensive and ridiculous form of permanent way, and a type of locomotive possessing no practical advantages, Mr Fell's plan is admirable".

*See illustration on cover.

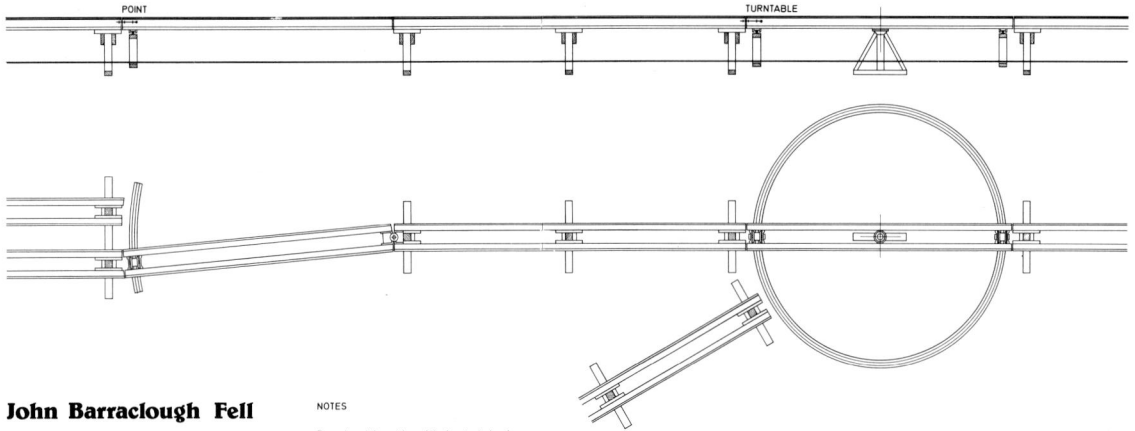

John Barraclough Fell
Patent No. 1246   1871

NOTES

Reproduced from the original patent drawing.

All moving sections located with sliding
bolts, shown thus: ••·••

POINT   TURNTABLE

TIPPLER   GATE

Sheet 1 of 2 sheets

NOT TO SCALE   © E.A.Wade 5/1978

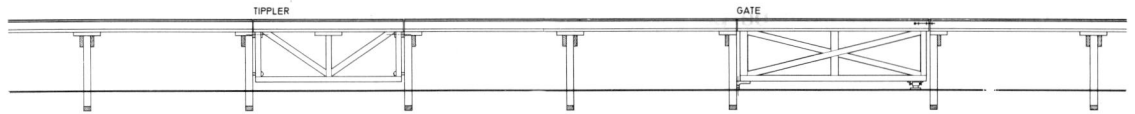

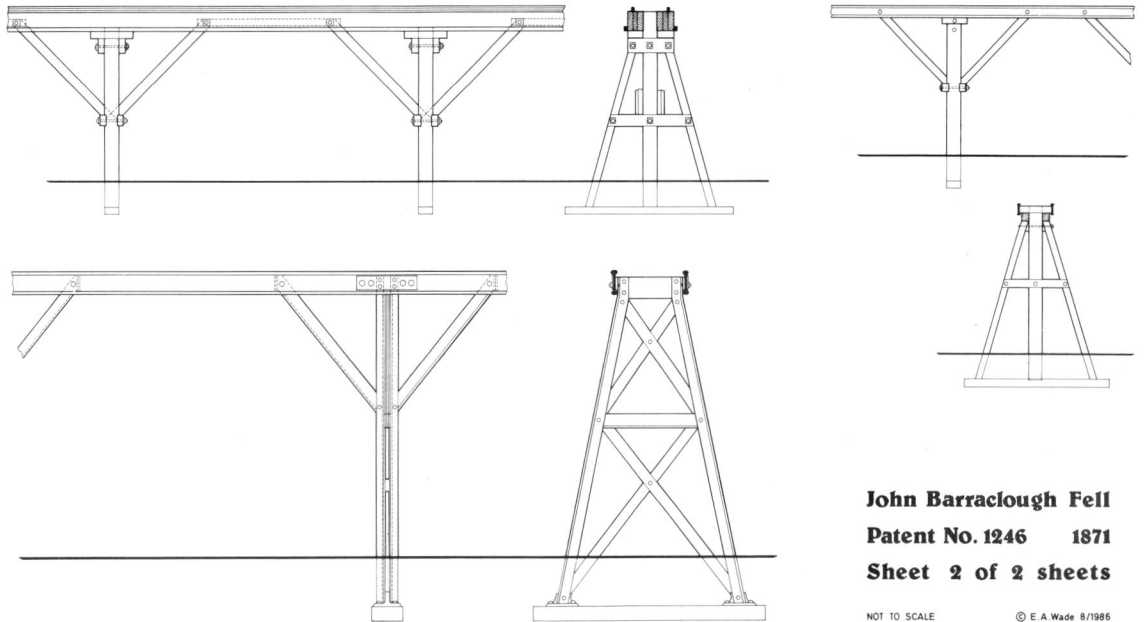

John Barraclough Fell
Patent No. 1246   1871
Sheet 2 of 2 sheets

NOT TO SCALE   © E.A.Wade 8/1986

"A HOPELESSLY INCONVENIENT AND RIDICULOUS PLAN"

A further patent followed, in May 1871, which further detailed the trackwork to be used on Fell's proposed locomotive worked railway system. This was basically a development and updating of the fourth part of his 'monorail' patent; the single rail system having been, by this time, more or less forgotten. It describes, in words and drawings, the method of track and trestle construction, in wood, iron, or a combination of the two. It goes on to describe the way in which switches, or points, would be constructed and the method of forming a turntable. The patent also details a tippler, by which means wagons could be tipped over, on a section of track, in order to unload them rapidly; and the method of constructing a gate to allow for the passage of road vehicles when the trackwork was at low level. All of these things will be best appreciated by reference to the accompanying drawings. The patent also covered the use of endless ropes as a means of powering such railways; a means which had been in use on the 8in gauge Parkhouse Mineral Railway for a year or so. The rope was to be held by a clamp or clip on the side of the train or wagon "but below the level of the guide wheels when used", and was guided around curves in the track by means of vertically positioned cylindrical rollers or pulleys.

At the request of the War Office, Fell constructed a mile of railway at the South Camp, Aldershot, in the first half of 1872. The Aldershot Railway (it is convenient to name it thus although there is no record of any official title ever having been bestowed) was laid to a gauge of 18 inches and was constructed in only forty five days; for the purpose of conveying stores to and from the Victualling Office.* The main purpose however, was to thoroughly test the viability of Fell's system. The line commenced at the Stores Department, near the town, and for some distance ran just above ground level, but climbing continually. It then curved sharply left and became a viaduct, 770ft long and 25ft high in the centre. The viaduct itself was quite straight but continued to rise at a gradient of 1 in 50. After leaving the viaduct, the line turned again to the left, through a small cutting, and ran close past the upper stores, bakery and meat store. This was the highest point on the railway and from there it curved first right and then left, gradually descending, until it reached the road near the Flagstaff hill; where it terminated. It was proposed to extend the railway to the North Camp and canvas camping ground, and to eventually connect it with the Basingstoke Canal and the London and South Western Railway. The Aldershot Railway was utilised to distribute stores through the camp but was never sufficiently extensive to do the job properly. At this time a large number of horses were employed in taking bread and meat from the South to the North Camp and in carrying all kinds of stores from the main line railway to the camp. Had the Fell railway been made better use of, many of these horses (which appear to have been hired) could have been dispensed with. The railway was built on the most direct route available and Fell made no attempt to avoid any natural difficulties. It was laid out much in the way that army engineers might construct such a line in time of war. The whole construction was of timber, with the obvious exception of the 30 lb/yd flat bottomed carrying rails, as may be seen in the accompanying drawings. All the trestle members were 8in x 4in, or 8in x 8in, and could be cut and drilled to a template in the sawmill with the assurance that they would all fit together on site. The bottom members of the truss simply rested on the ground in the same way as a normal railway sleeper.** It will be noted that the guide rails were of hardwood although the sub-committee of the Royal Engineers Committee had recommended that they be of iron. The 'points' on the Aldershot Railway had a 20ft long pivoting section, and conformed to the design shown in the patent.

A locomotive to work the railway was built in accordance with Fell's patents by Manning, Wardle and Co. of Leeds. Works number 412, she carried the name ARIEL on a brass plate and was dispatched from the works on 10 July 1872. She had outside cylinders of 6.1/2in bore and 10in stroke, mounted on the side frames, which were carried down below rail level. She ran on six coupled wheels, with steel axles and tyres, of 1ft 4in diameter. The wheelbase was 10ft 8in and the centre pair of wheels were flangeless in order to permit the locomotive to pass around tighter curves. It has been stated elsewhere that all six driving wheels were flangeless, which would be possible as she was fitted with guide wheels, but the maker's drawings show this

*The line is said to have cost about £2,000 without rolling stock.

**Sir Arthur Heywood, in his book *Minimum Gauge Railways*, refers to a viaduct he built in 1878 as "an improvement upon one at Aldershot, put up by a gentleman who induced the War Office to sanction a short experimental line for army transport upon a hopelessly inconvenient and ridiculous plan".

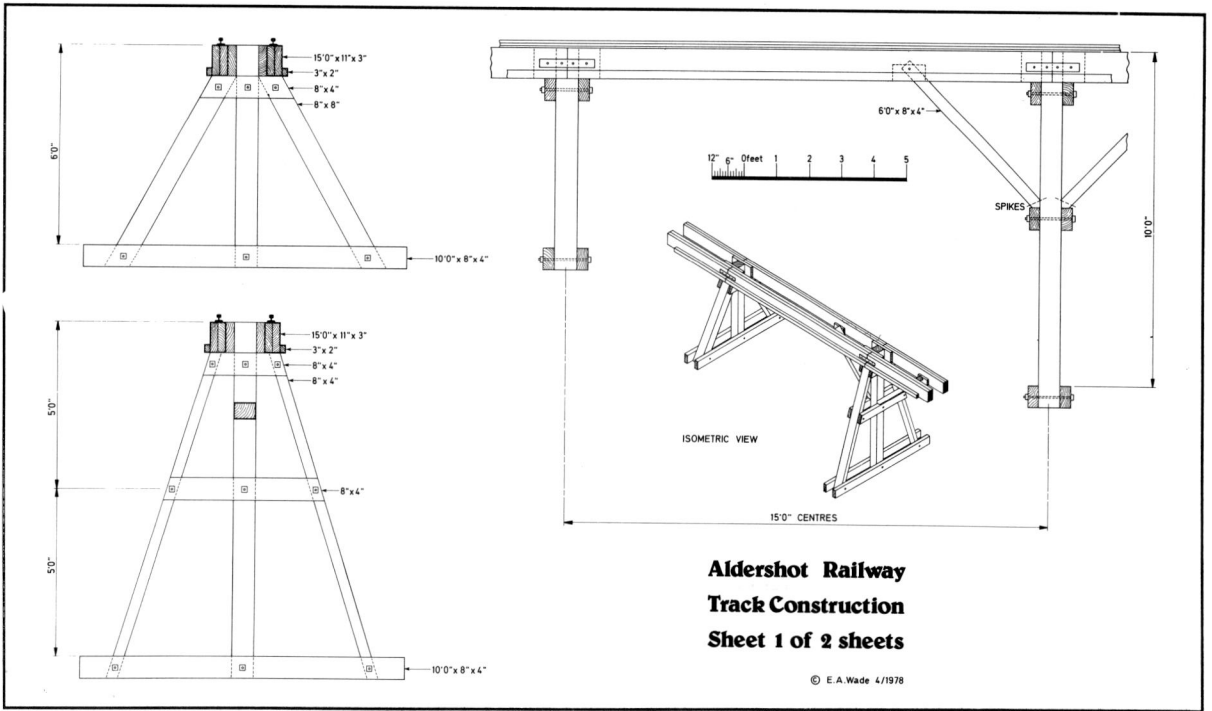

15'0" x 11" x 3"
3" x 2"
8" x 4"
8" x 8"

6'0"

6'0" x 8" x 4"

SPIKES

10'0"

10'0" x 8" x 4"

12" 6" 0feet 1 2 3 4 5

ISOMETRIC VIEW

15'0" x 11" x 3"
3" x 2"
8" x 4"
8" x 4"

5'0"

8" x 4"

5'0"

10'0" x 8" x 4"

15'0" CENTRES

Aldershot Railway
Track Construction
Sheet 1 of 2 sheets

© E.A.Wade 4/1978

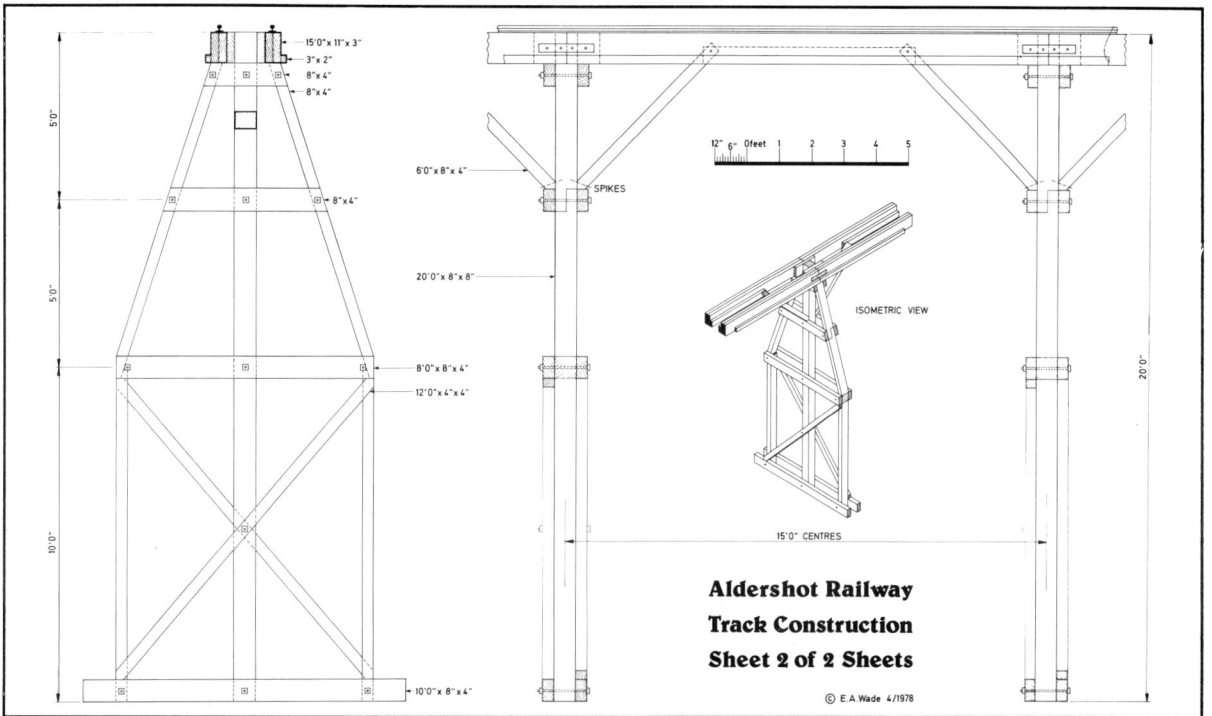

15'0" x 11" x 3"
3" x 2"
8" x 4"
8" x 4"

5'0"

6'0" x 8" x 4"

SPIKES

8" x 4"

20'0" x 8" x 8"

12" 6" 0feet 1 2 3 4 5

ISOMETRIC VIEW

5'0"

8'0" x 8" x 4"
12'0" x 4" x 4"

20'0"

10'0"

10'0" x 8" x 4"

15'0" CENTRES

Aldershot Railway
Track Construction
Sheet 2 of 2 Sheets

© E.A.Wade 4/1978

11

not to have been the case. The boiler was of interest at the time in that it was welded and flanged and the firebox was of copper, with a heating surface of only 14 sq.ft. Twenty-two brass boiler tubes (of 1.7/8in outside diameter) gave a heating surface of 62 sq.ft; making a total heating surface of 76 sq.ft, with a grate area of only about 3 sq.ft. Water was supplied to the boiler by two injectors. The locomotive weighted 4 tons 8.1/2cwt. ARIEL was supplied with a tender which ran upon four flanged wheels of 1ft 4in diameter, all of which were braked; no brakes being fitted to the locomotive. The wheelbase was 8ft 2in, the water tank held 172 gallons and the fuel capacity was 15 cubic feet. In working order it weighted 3 tons 15.1/2cwt; giving a total weight for engine and tender of 8 tons 4 cwt, distributed over a total wheelbase of 22ft 5in.

Both engine and tender were supplied with flanged horizontal guide wheels (which were unpowered) and a handrail was provided around the extremities of the locomotive so that the driver might safely move around her whilst she was in motion. *The Engineer* for 1 November 1872 (a journal that was kinder than *Engineering*) said of ARIEL, "The little engine is beautifully made, and does her work very well indeed; but the cylinders are placed too low, a defect which will be remedied in a second engine now in course of construction".*

The ten wagons which ran on the Aldershot Railway were 13ft long with bodies 8ft long by 5ft 6in wide by 2ft deep. The body was made of 2.1/2in planking strengthened with 1/4in thick plates of iron at the corners. They ran on six wheels, also of 1ft 4in diameter, and had a wheelbase of 10ft. The

*This second engine was PENTEWAN, of the 2ft 6in gauge Pentewan Railway in Cornwall, which left the works of Manning, Wardle in 1873. She was outwardly very similar to ARIEL and did indeed carry her cylinders in a more orthodox position, but she was never intended to carry guide wheels; having been designed according to a slightly different set of principals which will be discussed in due course.

Fell's locomotive for the Aldershot Railway, from The Engineer, *1 November 1872.*

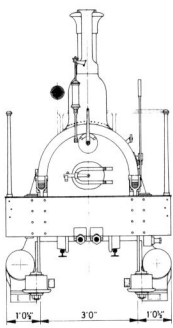

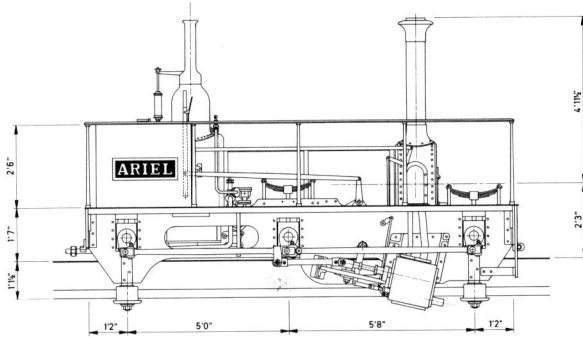

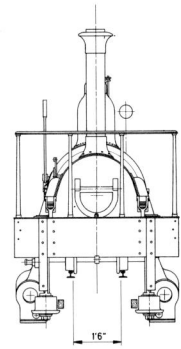

Sheet 1 of 2 sheets

NOTES

Reproduced from maker's drawings and photographic evidence.

Smokebox and firebox doors are conjectural but based on Manning Wardle practice of the period.

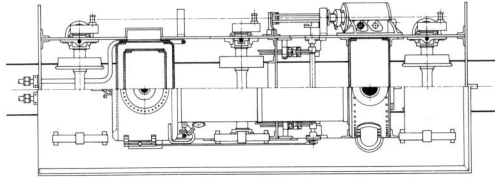

12" 6" 0feet 1 2 3 4 5

Manning Wardle & Co
Works number ~ 412
0-6-0Ten. Built 1872

'ARIEL' of the Aldershot Railway
Cylinders - 6¼"bore x 10"stroke   Gauge - 1'6"
Wheel diameter - 1'4"
Weight in working order - 4tons 8cwt 2qrs
Boiler pressure - not recorded
© E.A.Wade 4/1978

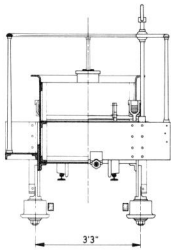

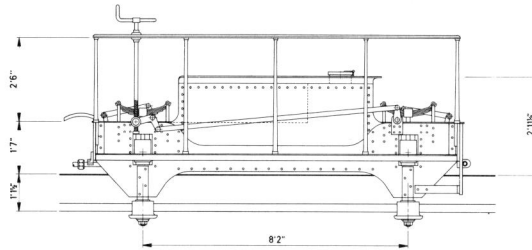

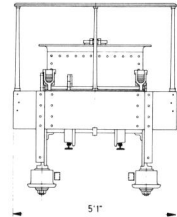

Sheet 2 of 2 sheets

NOTES

Reproduced from known dimensions and photographic evidence.

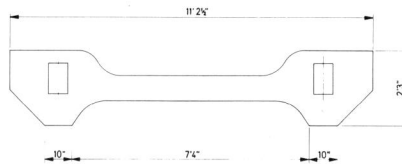

12" 6" 0feet 1 2 3 4 5

Manning Wardle & Co
Works number ~ 412
0-6-0Ten. Built 1872

Tender for 'ARIEL' of the Aldershot Railway
Wheel diameter - 1'4"   Gauge - 1'6"
Weight in working order - 3tons 15cwt 2qrs
Tank capacity - 172 gallons
Bunker capacity - 15cu ft
© E.A.Wade 4/1978

side frames (made of oak, 10in deep by 5in wide) also formed the buffers and were suspended from the axles by bolts passing through two volute springs fixed on each pedestal; the pedestal rising and falling with the action of the springs. Thus, the bottom of the wagon was brought within 3in of rail level and the centre of gravity, for an empty wagon, was some 8in above the rails. Each wagon was fitted with four horizontal flanged guide wheels and Fell claimed that their stability was equal to that found on a 3ft 6in flanged railway. A draw bar passed under the centre of the wagon with a draw lock and chain attached to it. The wagons weighed 30 cwt and could each carry a load of 4 tons, or from 300 to 400 cubic feet of bulky goods, or even 500 cubic feet of light material, such as hay. They could also carry twelve men in marching order. The railway was also said to be capable of carrying 7 ton siege guns, between two wagons.

The 15 November 1872 edition of *The Engineer* contained illustrations of the wagons and of a passenger carriage; both of which are somewhat out of proportion when compared to the given dimensions. The underframe and wheels of the carriage were constructed in the same way as the wagons and the passengers were to sit facing one another. It seems unlikely that a passenger carriage was ever constructed, but obviously the design had been finalised. The body was to be 12ft long, 5ft 6in wide and 6ft high above the floor. The centre of the roof was raised in a clerestory, which contained lights and ventilators and also gave headroom for walking through from the end balconies. The sides were kept deliberately low in order to reduce the centre of gravity. These carriages would have seated twelve first class passengers or fourteen second or third class and would have weighed from 1.1/2 to 2tons each. It was also envisaged that the passengers might be seated back to back "after the fashion of an Irish car". In such a case, the seats could have been brought down to rail level and the floor of the carriage lowered to the level of the guide wheels. On 25 November, a certain W.T. wrote a letter to the Editor of *The Engineer* (published 13 December 1872) in which he stated, "The question is, what security exists in the construction of these vehicles against accidents due to the breaking of axles or to the liberation of the axle from the pedestals or axle boxes? Judging from your illustration of the carriage this risk has not been guarded against. If such is the case, I would suggest that the idea of suspension might receive a severe shock some fine morning".

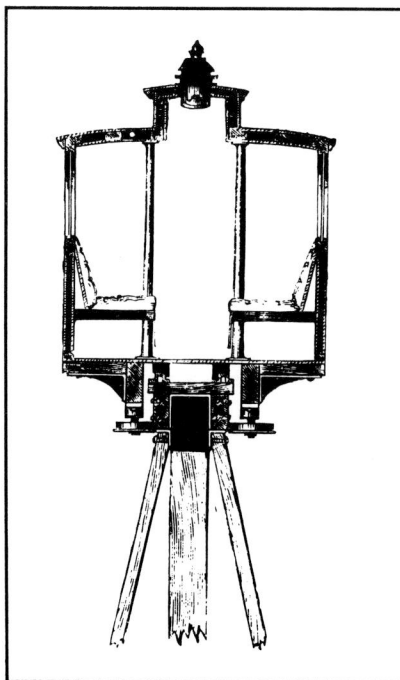

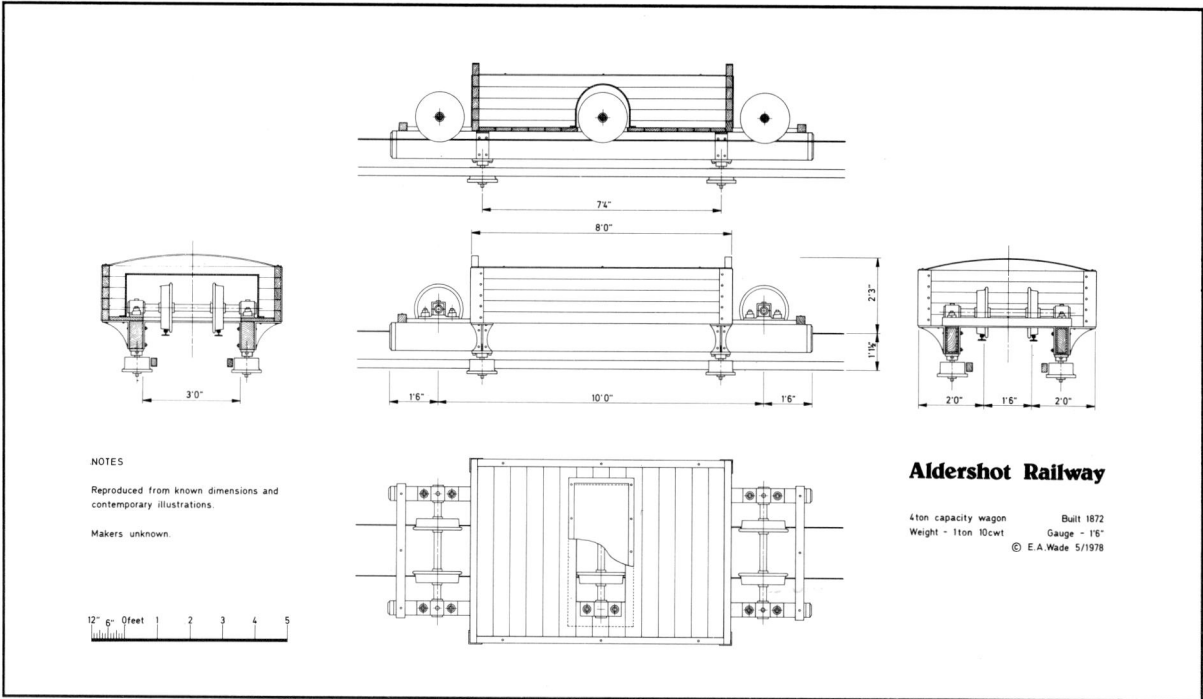

NOTES

Reproduced from known dimensions and
contemporary illustrations.

Makers unknown.

Aldershot Railway

4 ton capacity wagon   Built 1872
Weight – 1 ton 10cwt   Gauge – 1'6"
© E.A.Wade 5/1978

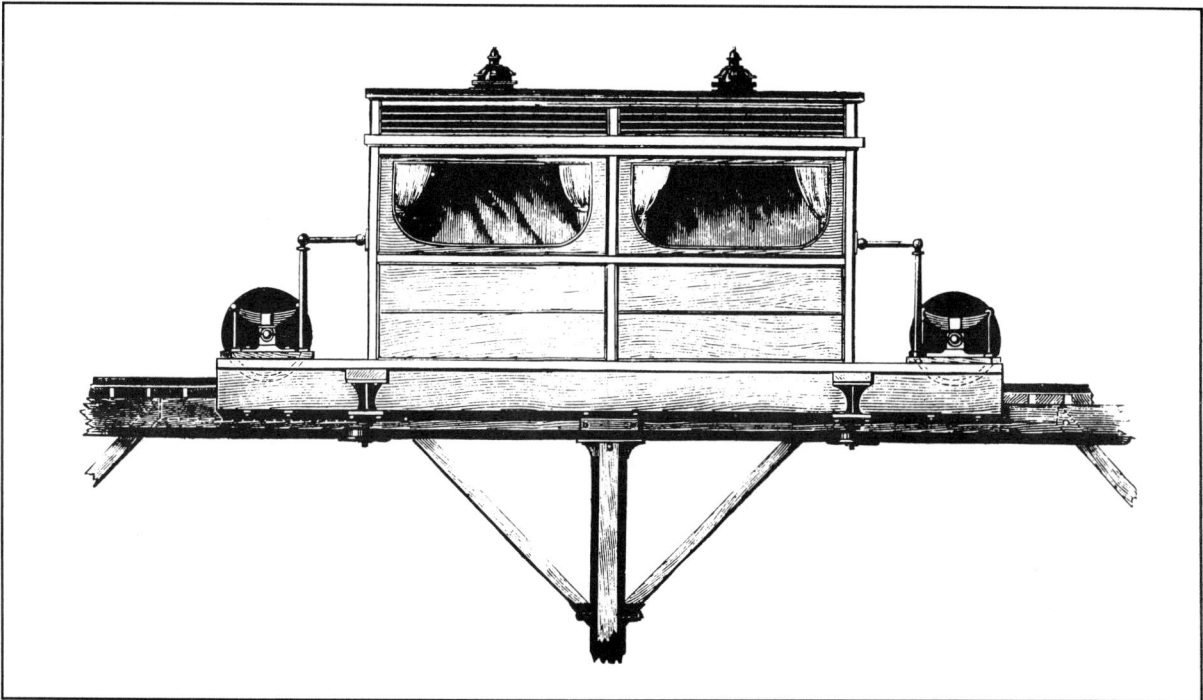

Carriage design for the Aldershot Railway. Note the method of track construction.

"ARDOUR IN THE PERSUIT OF SCIENCE"

Once the Aldershot Railway was complete, the Inspector General of Fortifications, General Sir F.E. Chapman, requested, on 25 July 1872, that a representative of the Royal Engineers Committee might go and inspect it, "preliminary to arranging a programme of experiments". The Committee duly sent their Secretary to make the inspection and, on 1 August, he submitted, with the Committee's approval, the programme of experiments to the Inspector General of Fortifications. The Inspector General approved the programme on 15 August but, following a request from Colonel Ogle, the Commanding Royal Engineer, Aldershot, they were postponed until after the autumn manoeuvres. The experiments were eventually carried out on 19 October 1872, when "The engine drew a load of 25 tons up the slope of 1 in 50 and ran with loads over the whole line easily, and with no more vibration in crossing a timber viaduct than is usually experienced in such structures". The experiments were carried out in the presence of: General Sir F.E. Chapman, Colonel Ogle, R.E., Colonel Somerset, R.E., Lieut.Colonel Chesney, R.E., and several other officers from the War Department. The wagon carried 590 cubic feet of hay and two others were loaded with soldiers carrying their rifles and complete equipment. The Royal Engineers Committee and other officers were carried in further wagons. Passenger carrying trains were run over the railway at twenty miles an hour, mixed trains at fifteen and goods trains at an average speed of ten miles an hour. The trains ran as steadily as any standard gauge train; even when a passenger train reached the maximum speed of thirty miles an hour. Further experiments were planned for 30 October, for the benefit of a group of engineers including, among many others, Captain Luard, R.E., Mr Wardle (of Manning, Wardle), J.B. Fell and his son, G.N. Fell. The locomotive, on this occasion, was driven by a Mr Barnes, who was the locomotive superintendant of the Mont Cenis Railway. In the event, the weather was so bad that only three trips each way were made, with the locomotive and two wagons in which rode, "the fifteen or twenty gentlemen whose ardour in the persuit of science was not to be baffled by a storm of wind and rain". The mile was run in an average time of five minutes and a speed of twenty five miles an hour was attained. They were impressed with the steadiness of the motion and noted that the guide wheels never touched their rails, except on sharp curves. They declared themselves prepared to travel on the line at forty miles an hour!

Fell had, however, proved only part of his claims and further, more exhaustive tests were to come. On 24 October 1872, the President of the Royal Engineers Committee suggested that it might be advisable "to take up and relay the railway in a new situation to test the time actually required for removing it and to provide for sidings". This relaying was approved on 12 December by the Inspector General of Fortifications who, in January 1873, received a letter from Fell relating to a proposed alteration in the mode of constructing the trestles. This alteration concerned the use of cast or wrought iron brackets, the latter being preferred by the Committee, and it would seem that these brackets were to be fitted at the juncture of the trestles with the main carrying beams. The trackwork shown in the illustration of the carriage suggests something of the sort. On the last day of January the Commanding Royal Engineer, Aldershot was given authority, following the recommendation of the Committee, to take up half a mile of the railway, alter the trestles as proposed by Fell and relay it towards the London and South Western Railway.

Nothing further happened until 27 March 1873 when Captain Luard, R.E. (who, for the purposes of these experiments, had been made an Associate Member of the Royal Engineers Committee) submitted a plan and memorandum about the alterations. The Committee wished "to take half the line as representing a finished part, and to have the other half relaid as it would be on service, using the completed part as the only feeder". They enquired how many men Fell proposed to use for the relaying and, in April, Fell answered them thus: 10 men for transport, 4 for digging and filling holes, 4 for erecting trestles, 4 for erecting beams, 4 for adjusting and fastening beams and 4 platelayers. This, plus one foreman, made a (provisional) total of 31 men per gang and eight gangs were envisaged for each half mile of track constructed in a working day. Thus 248 men would be employed per half mile and a staff of one superintendent and one assistant made a round figure of 250; or 500 men per mile per day. However, at the end of May, Captain Luard notified the Committee that the Lieut. General Commanding at Aldershot would not sanction the employment of the necessary number of men during the drill season but was prepared to lay (or relay) half a mile with a gang of sappers. The Committee agreed to this and 9 June was fixed for the experiment. Fell requested several days for the men to practice their work, without actually laying the rails, before the Committee witnessed it. He proposed to move the timbers by means of "two wheels with axle and pole...with one horse...without the wheels probably double the number of carriers would be required". The Committee noted Fell's intention to be abroad for three weeks after Easter.

Captain Luard provided the Committee with an estimate of the works as follows:

ESTIMATE

For one mile of Fell's Railway, with bays of 10' beams 10" x 5" it has been calculated that an average height of 3'9" trestle contains 5.1/2 cubic feet of timber.
Each pair of carrying beams contain 7 cubic feet of timber. In one mile there are 528 bays, and the guide rails for one mile contain 440 cubic feet of timber.

	£	s	d
528 (5.1/2+7)+440+5.1/2 = 7045 cubic feet of timber @ 2s	704	10	0
Bolts of various lengths, nuts, fishplates,&c., 2 tons @ £20	40	0	0
Cast iron brackets-528 pairs @3s 6d a pair	92	8	0
Rails (20lbs) 3.1/2 tons @ £24	378	0	0
Dogs, dog nails, spikes, &c., 1.1.2 tons@ £24	36	0	0
Labour in preparing structure(military labour)	40	0	0
Labour in laying (military labour)	34	0	0
Carriage of materials	20	0	0
	£1344	18	0
Add for contingencies and royalty	55	0	0
Total	£1400	0	0

One gang of 29 men was employed in the experiment, their duties being divided as per Fell's requirements except that only 9 were used to transport the materials. Work commenced at 11.51 am and eight lengths of trestles and beams were laid before they stopped for dinner at 12.51; although the rails were not spiked down. They restarted at 2.20 and, by 4.50, all the trestles, beams and rails were laid out in position. At 5pm ten men stopped work. The 33rd trestle was completed by 5.18, "making up the work for 10 hours according to Mr Fell's estimate, and by 5.50, 38 trestles were in position with the rails completed as far as the 34th.

It was found that, when the locomotive stood in the centre of a bay 10ft long (said to be constructed of scantling 10in x 5in although the original structure was of two thicknesses, 11in x 3in)* deflection was found to be 1/4in. The timber guide rails, which should have been nailed to the beams as part of the prefabrication, had been omitted but the time taken to fit them was not counted in the experiment. The threads on the ends of some bolts were burred from rough handling and it was suggested that a slight tapering would obviate the difficulty experienced in screwing on the nuts. A point was also constructed, having a length of 29ft 6in, the diverging lines of which were at 3ft 8.1/2in centres.

These proceedings might be thought to have amply supported the claims which Fell had made for his railway system and the requirements set down by the military; despite the limited extent of the second set of experiments. However, from this point the Committee started to hesitate and have second thoughts about the whole project. In September 1873 the Secretary to the Committee submitted that, if further experiments were required, sufficient men would be available following the end of the drill season and the Committee asked Fell if he could show them an example of his railway system on "rough and rocky ground". Fell stated that "the part of his railway near St. Austell which runs over rough and rocky ground" had not yet commenced construction but that he would inform them when it did. This line, the Pentewan Railway, partly represents the next stage in the development of Fell's ideas, which require some attention at this point as they partially account for the demise of Fell's plans for rapidly constructed military railways on the guide rail principle, as epitomised by Aldershot.

*The original line had also been constructed with 15ft bays.

"SO LIGHT A STRUCTURE COMBINED WITH SAFETY"

Fell registered four further patents (in 1873, 1879, 1880 and 1882 - the first being a joint patent with his son George Noble Fell) dealing with what we may term elevated narrow gauge railways **without** guide rails. These patents deal both with trackwork and locomotives and it is convenient to consider these two aspects separately. The trackwork was, in most essentials, similar to the track used at Aldershot in that it was constructed of beams and trestles, in wood or iron; resulting in a railway which ran at varying heights above ground level. The same benefits were claimed; speed, ease and cheapness of construction resulting from prefabrication and minimal earthworks. The only important difference was the absence of guide rails. This was not because Fell had lost faith or interest in the guide wheel principle but because his new system was for (to quote from the 1873 patent) "light railways of any gauge, but generally of gauges of two feet and upwards"; whereas the guide rail principle had been (and still was) intended for gauges of 15 or 18 inches where the greatly increased stability justified the additional cost. As Fell was now seeking "improvements in the construction" of the more common and larger sizes of narrow gauge railway, it is not surprising that, with each successive patent, he sought to strengthen the method of track construction. Any weaknesses in his earlier designs were no doubt revealed by the study of those examples which were actually built. It should also be noted that the patents envisaged the possible use of Fell's centre rail traction on such lines; which further illustrates how each of Fell's patents built on the preceeding ones, rather than supplanting them.

Early in 1873 (at the time, be it noted, when the first of these four patents was being registered) Fell was appointed engineer to the newly formed Pentewan Railway and Harbour Co Ltd, of Cornwall, which had been formed to rebuild the old horse drawn Pentewan Railway and drag it into the locomotive era. An excellent history of the Pentewan has been written by Dr M.J.T. Lewis which needs no comment from the present writer other than with relation to Fell and his patents; an area in which Dr Lewis seems to be somewhat confused. As the Pentewan was being rebuilt (to a gauge of 2ft 6in) rather than constructed anew, a useable trackbed for a conventional railway was already in existence. Thus the case for an elevated line on Fell's trestles could hardly be convincingly argued although, as Dr Lewis shows, it appears to have been seriously suggested. However, Dr Lewis assumes that the suggestion was for a line on the guide rail principle, although he produces no evidence to substantiate this assumption. It seems far more likely that Fell aimed at using the Pentewan Railway as a proving ground for the latest development of his ideas, as detailed in the 1873 patent, and no doubt his appointment as an engineer to the line had some responsibility for his ideas developing as they did. Proposed extensions to the railway were certainly planned with Fell's elevated trackwork (without any suggestion of guide rails) but were unfortunately never built. The system was, of course, quite compatible with ground level track as future developments elsewhere were to show. In the event, the only example of Fell trackwork to be erected at Pentewan was the trestle viaduct used for unloading in the harbour.

The one real example of Fell's system of track construction sans guide rails came in 1880 (one year after the second of Fell's relevant patents) with the building of the 3ft gauge Torrington and Marland Railway in North Devon; to which Fell was also the engineer. Much of it was built as a conventional ground level railway but in its length there were ten Fell viaducts; although some of these were very small. In a conventional railway the route is planned so that the earth removed from cuttings equals the earth needed to build embankments. In replacing embankments with his timber viaducts, Fell obviated the need for cuttings so that the line could now follow the contours of the land. Hence, the need for earthworks was minimal. The line was opened on 5 February 1881 and was a little over 6 miles in length. An account of the inaugural trip over the line appeared in the *Bideford Weekly Gazette* which remarked, "On...getting on to the slender looking bridge, right above the river Torridge, and from thence on to a timber viaduct, 266 yards in length, and forty feet in height, the feeling of jollity suddenly changed to one of wonder and tremulation - wonder that engineering skill could devise so light a structure combined with safety, and tremulation lest the one thought uppermost in the minds of all should be realised". The bridge, as well as the viaducts, was built precisely in accordance with the patents and may be seen in the illustrations. A very well researched history of the T&MR appears in M.J. Messenger's book *North Devon Clay*, in which we learn of a visit to the line by the Secretary of the Chinese Legation in London with a view to building such lines in his own country. Also present amongst the party was a Major Grover, R.E., from the War Office.

Two views of Fell's bridge over the River Torridge and the viaducts leading to it.
These structures are built in accordance with his patents of 1873 and 1879.
(M.J. Messenger)

The viaduct leading to the bridge over the Torridge whilst under construction. Note the absence of handrails. (Collection E.A. Wade)

Marland Line and Furzebeam Hill, Torrington 464 over Torrington

The other end of the Torridge viaduct and its connection to a ground level section of line. (M.J. Messenger)

Mr Messenger devotes a chapter to J.B. Fell and his viaducts and informs us that, "they served the line for more than forty years", which is sufficient comment on the soundness of the engineering. Tests carried out on the supporting trestles of Fell viaducts showed them to be capable of supporting 50 tons, whereas the greatest load ever imposed would be the weight of one locomotive; about 9 tons. Mr Messenger also states that, "The six mile line was completed, almost, in the six months laid down for its construction and although the cost was 50% more than the tender the final cost of £2,400 per mile was still very economical". Mr Messenger deals with that part of Fell's work which is relevant to his subject with great finesse but is guilty of an inaccuracy when he states, as does Dr Lewis (twice) that the guide wheels on the Aldershot Railway were discarded as being unnecessary. These wheels, which were never utilised for tractive purposes, did no real work and indeed only touched the guide rails at corners. They were fitted, however, to provide both stability and safety on very narrow gauges (which, to judge from the Parkhouse accident, they did very well) and the present writer knows of no evidence of their ever being removed.

Let us know turn to Fell's developing ideas for locomotives as described in this final group of four patents and the realisation of these ideas on the two above mentioned railways. His earlier patents, for the guide wheel system, had envisaged a type of locomotive in which the centre of gravity was kept very low by placing the driving wheels in front of the smokebox and behind the firebox; the resulting long wheelbase being utilised to spread the load on the lightly constructed elevated trackwork. The axle loading was also decreased by a third pair of driving wheels (necessarily flangeless) under the boiler and the use of tenders to carry coal and water. The centre of gravity could be lowered still further, as in ARIEL, by placing the cylinders below rail level. These ideas were retained with the exception of the last one, which was clearly impossible on a railway system which used conventional points. However, Fell developed the theme by proposing powered tenders articulated with the locomotives, thus spreading the load over six pairs of driven wheels. One design

Torridge viaduct from the south. The timber structure and handrails have been enhanced in ink on this hand-tinted postcard. (Collection J.B. Horne)

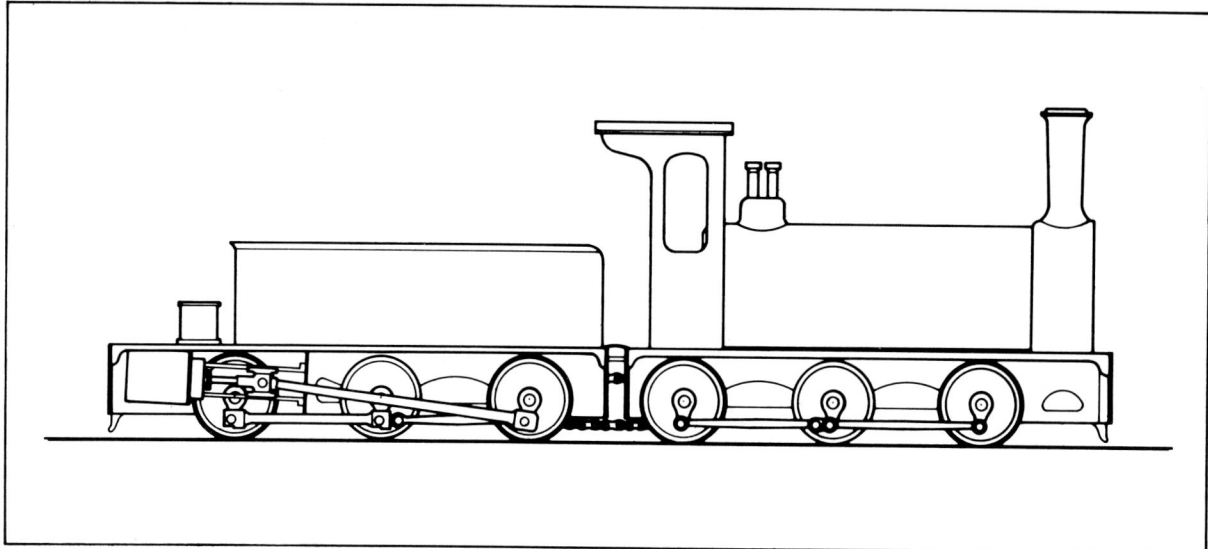

ARTICULATED LOCOMOTIVE from patent number 3579 of 1882

PENTEWAN standing on Fell's trestle viaduct in Pentewan harbour.   (Locomotive Publishing Co)

even had eight pairs, four of which were flangeless! He stated that, "By this arrangement the size and power of the engine may be increased without increasing the weight per lineal foot of structure". He also proposed radial axles, flexible steam pipes, the coupling of two engines back to back with flexible coupling rods! There is also the inevitable drawing to illustrate how such a locomotive would incorporate centre rail traction.

The locomotives which were actually built were not so adventurous and number only five. The first was PENTEWAN, of the Pentewan Railway, which was built by Manning, Wardle and Co in 1873 (works number 461) to Fell's own design, at a cost of £925. This locomotive was very similar to ARIEL, which is not really surprising as they were both designed by Fell within a year of each other, they had the same builders and were designed on the same principles. This similarity has led people to assume that PENTEWAN (and hence the Pentewan Railway) was intended to be fitted with guide wheels but this was never the case, as the maker's drawings illustrate. Like ARIEL she had a very low slung boiler and the firebox dropped between the second and third axles to keep the centre of gravity as low as possible. Unlike ARIEL she, necessarily, had her cylinders in the conventional position and the smokebox was placed low in front of the leading axle, rather than behind it. Consequently, although PENTEWAN was the larger engine (7in x 12in cylinders as against 6.1/2in x 10in) she had the shorter wheelbase (10ft 0in to ARIEL's 10ft 8in). The total wheelbase, with tender, was also shorter (18ft 6in to 22ft 5in). Nevertheless, the wheelbase was still long enough to necessitate flangeless centre wheels and, as with the earlier locomotive, the weight was distributed further by the use of a tender. This tender was of conventional design and considerably shorter and taller than ARIEL's and there must be some doubt as to whether it was designed by Fell. Once again, brakes were only fitted to the tender. PENTEWAN was clearly an adaption of a proven design for what he hoped would be the first railway built to his non-guide rail system and she predates his additional concepts for locomotives on such lines, as detailed in his patents.

PENTEWAN cannot have been considered unsuccessful for she was replaced, in 1886, by TREWITHEN (Manning, Wardle works number 994) which was, but for the addition of an ornate cab, almost identical. TREWITHEN was a little cheaper (£774) as she inherited PENTEWAN's tender. Other differences included a slightly larger boiler and cylinders of 1/2in larger bore. One significant difference was the provision of compensation levers between the springs to the leading and centre axles. Locomotives of such long wheelbase would have inevitably suffered from the poorly maintained trackwork of the Pentewan Railway and these compensation levers appear to have been an attempt to cure a problem found with the earlier engine. They may not have done the trick for TREWITHEN also had a short life; being retired in 1901. She was sold for scrap, along with PENTEWAN, which had been lying idle for years, in the summer of 1903. It is worth noting that they were replaced by a third locomotive from Manning, Wardle; which suggests that the railway company was satisfied with the standard of their products. This third engine was not built to Fell's design (Fell by this time being retired) but it should be noted that it was ordered in a hurry when TREWITHEN was found to be in need of extensive repairs. Perhaps Manning, Wardle produced a partially completed locomotive from stock rather than taking the time to start from scratch.

The Torrington and Marland Railway owned three locomotives which were influenced by Fell, the line's engineer, to the extent that they all had long wheelbases (9ft 0in in each case) with flangeless centre wheels. This was necessary to spread the load on the timber viaducts. That feature apart, however, they were all quite conventional six- coupled tank locomotives with no attempt being made to lower the centre of gravity or spread their weight further by the use of tenders. The locomotives were: Black, Hawthorn & Co Ltd, number 576 of 1880; W.G. Bagnall, number 566 of 1883 and Avonside Engine Co, number 1428 of 1901. Perhaps, by 1880, Fell had realised that the centre of gravity was not so critical on a gauge as wide as 3ft. Certainly, the locomotives outlined in his last patent for the non-guide rail system (1882) do not appear to be particularly low slung.

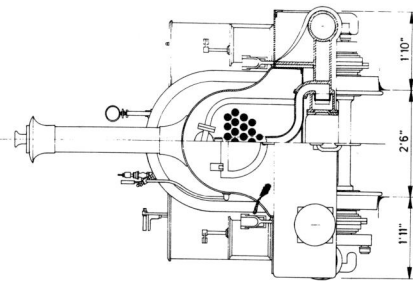

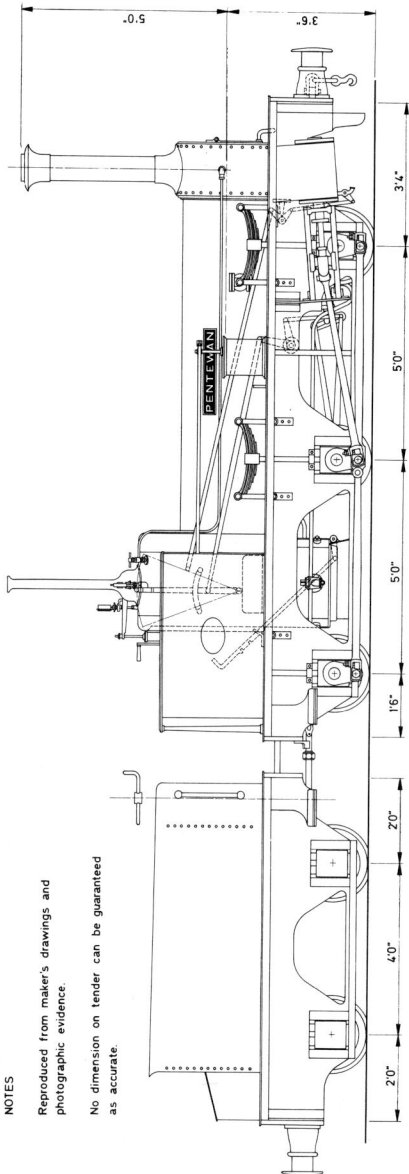

Manning Wardle & Co. — 461
Works No. 461
0-6-0Ten. Built 1873

'PENTEWAN' of the Pentewan Railway
Cylinders - 7"bore x 12"stroke   Gauge - 2'6"
Wheel diameter - 1'8"
Weight empty (engine only) - 6tons 10cwt 3qrs
Boiler pressure - not recorded

© E.A.Wade 3/1977

PENTEWAN

1'10"
2'6"
1'11"

5'0"
3'6"

3'4"
5'0"
5'0"
1'6"

2'0"
4'0"
2'0"

NOTES

Reproduced from maker's drawings and
photographic evidence.

No dimension on tender can be guaranteed
as accurate.

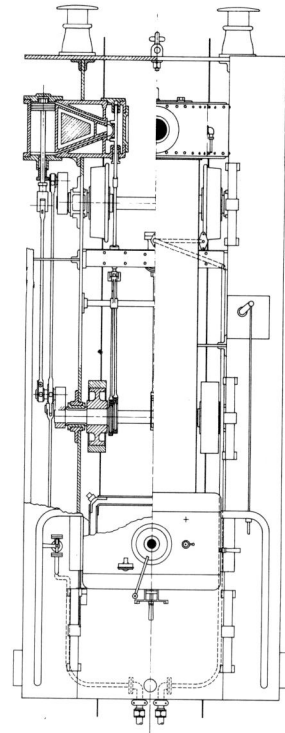

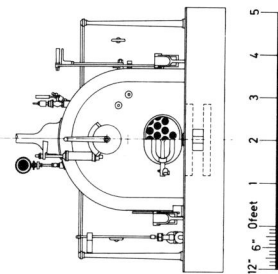

12" 6" 0feet 1 2 3 4 5

PENTEWAN *may be seen more clearly in this enlargement of the previous photograph.* (P.J.T. Reed)

Manning, Wardle and Co 994 of 1886 TREWITHEN at Pentawan Harbour.
The combination of a large cab with such a long, low boiler resulted in a
distinctive locomotive. (Locomotive Publishing Co)

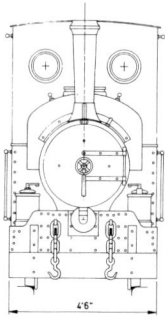

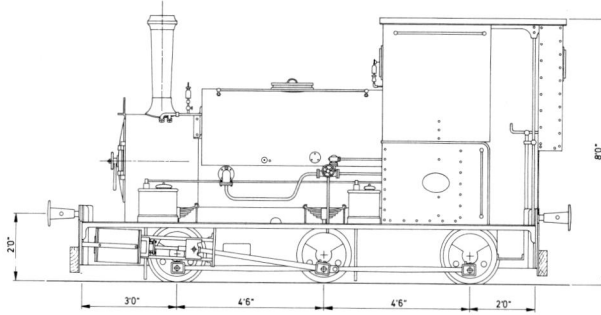

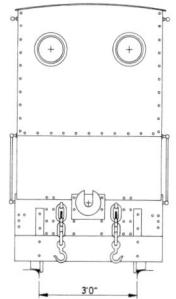

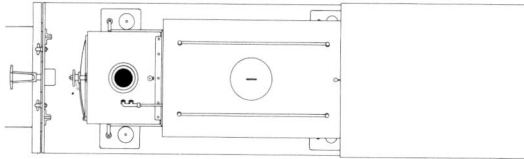

12" 6" 0feet 1 2 3 4 5

Black, Hawthorn
Works No. – 576
0-6-0T Built 1880

Cylinders - 7⅞"bore x 10"stroke   Gauge - 3'0"
Wheel diameter - 1'8"   (centre flangeless)
© E.A.Wade 8/1981

Black, Hawthorn 576 of 1880 (MARY) outside the engine shed on the Torrington and Marland Railway; after her meagre weather protection had been upgraded.   (L.C.G.B.)

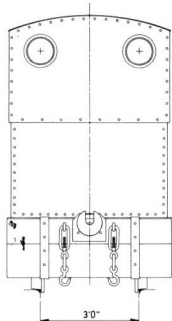

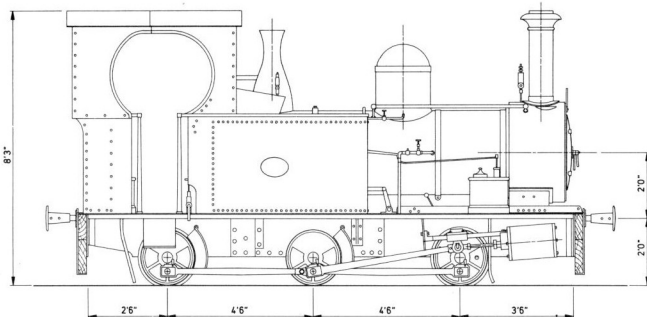

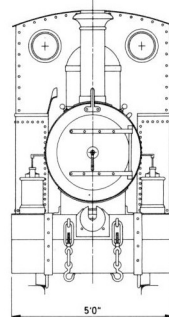

W.G.Bagnall, Ltd.
Works No. — 566
0-6-0T   Built 1883

Cylinders - 7⅛"bore x 10"stroke   Gauge - 3'0"
Wheel diameter - 1'8" (centre flangeless)
© E.A.Wade 9/1981

NOTES

This drawing is reconstructed from photographs as no drawings are extant. No
dimension can be guaranteed as accurate.

Safety chains omitted from side elevation.

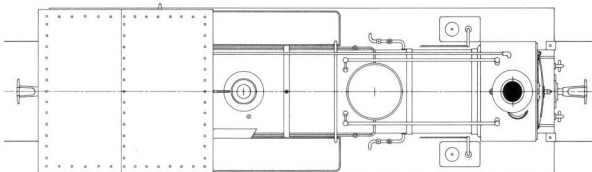

8'3"

3'0"

2'6"   4'6"   4'6"   3'6"

2'0"

2'0"

5'0"

12" 6" 0feet 1   2   3   4   5

W.G.Bagnall 566 of 1883 (MARLAND) in original condition, posed on one of Fell's viaducts on the T&MR. This viaduct, constructed in a mixture of timber and iron, conforms in every particular to a drawing in Fell's patent of 1880 (No 1249)

(E.A. Holwill)

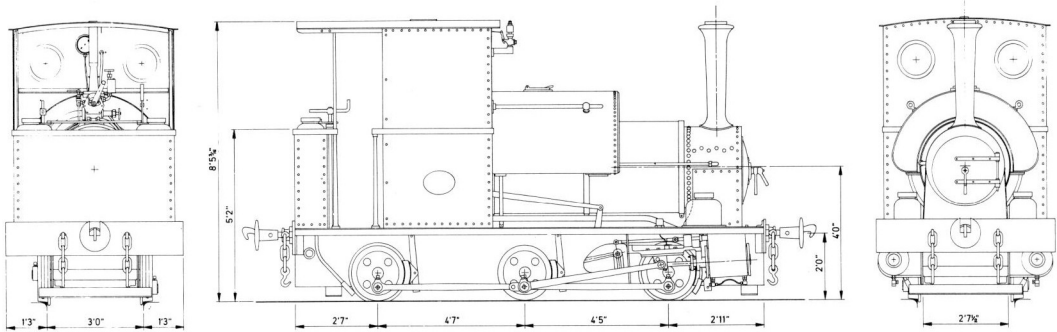

NOTES

Based on maker's drawings and photographic evidence.

Wheel bearings and springs omitted from end elevations.

Brakes and valve gear omitted from plan.

Avonside Engine Co
Works No. - 1428
0-6-0T Built 1901

Cylinders - 7"bore x 10"stroke   Gauge - 3'0"
Wheel diameter - 1'8"   (centre flangeless)
Weight in working order -   8 tons 12 cwt
Boiler pressure - 150 p.s.i.
Tank capacity - 130 gallons
© E.A.Wade 8/1981

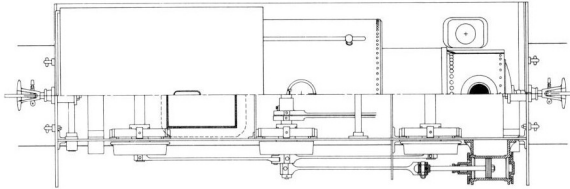

The manufacturer's photograph of Avonside Engine Co 1428 of 1901 (AVONSIDE), the last Fell inspired narrow gauge locomotive to be built.
(B.D. Stoyel)

"I CANNOT BE CONSIDERED RESPONSIBLE"

We may now return to consider events at Aldershot, subsequent to the two sets of experiments, which would appear to have fully justified all the claims which Fell had made for his guide rail system and, indeed, the requirements specified by the War Office. In February 1874, the Royal Engineers Committee requested the commanding officer at Aldershot "to suggest a line in which the whole railway could be relaid after taking down the part now standing. The new line to be considered irrespective of its utility in the camp, and simply as to the rate of laying it". Whether this was a serious proposal for further experiments, or a way of avoiding making a decision on the project, is open to question. Nevertheless, a survey was undertaken and drawings of the proposed line produced by the School of Military Engineering.

At this stage (27 March 1874) the Committee, having noted the development of Fell's ideas as illustrated by his 1873 patent and his involvement with the Pentewan Railway, wrote to ask if he was abandoning guide wheels "for commercial lines of railway". They also wrote to Captain Tyler (of the Railway Inspectorate) asking, "if he knows of any engines, &c., in use in England, which would be suitable for military field railways, lightness being an object". Fell replied, explaining that he was only giving up guide wheels in the larger gauges and when a large proportion of the railway was on the ground, "as on the St. Austell and Pentewan line". He also mentioned that he was, "now preparing plans for a short line with guide wheels in Fifeshire"! Captain Tyler replied that "light tank engines of the ordinary gauge would always be procurable for military purposes" and, on 30 April, he attended a meeting of the Committee which had been called to discuss the whole subject. On 5 June 1874 the Committee sent their report to the Inspector General of Fortifications. The report began: "The Committee have the honour to report that after full consideration of the question of the probable utility of Fell's railway for military purposes they are not prepared to recommend any further expenditure, or experiments with it, for the following reasons". The report then gives a resume of the advantages claimed for Fell's system, the appointment of the sub-committee and its visit to the Parkhouse Mineral Railway and the subsequent erection of the Aldershot Railway; all of which has been detailed above. The report to this point is impartial, other than to admit that the Parkhouse line, "had all the advantages, as regards facility of construction, simplicity, and stability, claimed for it".

However, the tone changes: "At the time the Committee recommended this trial, there appeared to be a reasonable prospect of Mr Fell's getting his side-wheel system into comparatively extended use in this country, in which case there would have been the necessary reserve of rolling stock available in the event of its being determined to make use of this kind of railway for an expedition. The experiments made at Aldershot have shown that a line on this system can be constructed at a very rapid rate, and have also suggested various improvements on the construction which might be introduced had the system come into comparatively extended use. Mr Fell has, however, practically abandoned the side-wheel system, and adopted in some cases a 2ft 6in gauge with no side wheels, which is in fact an ordinary narrow-gauge line, where the country is flat, and an ordinary narrow-gauge line on trestles, where the country is broken. While admitting that Mr Fell is quite right to adopt this change of system, where it is more applicable, the Committee cannot lose sight of the fact, that unless Mr Fell adheres to his original system and gets it into comparatively extended use, there will be no chance of obtaining the necessary rolling stock in any time likely to be available for getting it ready; and as this does not appear probable, they are not prepared to recommend any further expenditure upon the experimental line.

The question of what sort of railway it would be best to adopt for any particular expedition is not before the Committee, but it is evident that it must to a great degree depend upon the possibility of obtaining a large amount of rolling stock in a short time, as well as upon the facilities for landing heavy weights at the place of disembarkation, the amount of labour available, the nature of the country, and other considerations. The Committee are of the opinion that if at any future time Mr Fell introduces his side-wheel system on a uniform narrow gauge to such an extent as to afford the necessary reserve of rolling stock, it may be expedient to resume the consideration of the question. It appears at present to the Committee to be best to utilize the rolling stock, the trestle work, and the permanent way materials (of the Aldershot Railway), so as to afford the means of instruction in connection with military railways on which the side-wheels are not employed, rather than to incur further expenditure in extending or experimenting upon the Fell railway in its present form. The existing railway is not either as regards its position, or its length, available for the service of the camp at Aldershot. In order to render it available for such service several more miles of railway would be required, and if it were contemplated to construct such an extension, and constantly to employ it for the conveyance of camp stores and materials, it would not be desirable to continue the use of side-wheels, and it would probably be better to increase the width of the gauge. The Committee do not consider it desirable to say more at present on this question, which would require, before any further proceedings could be adopted, full discussion with the military authorities concerned".

Fell's response to this report is encapsulated in a letter of 3 April 1875 to the Inspector General of Fortifications: "Sir, Referring to my recent letters on the subject of the narrow-gauge railway at Aldershot, I have the honour to call your attention to the experiments which have been made on that railway in the years 1872 and 1873, and to ask you to allow me to be furnished with a copy of the report of the Royal Engineers Committee upon the two series of trials which have been made.

"The object of the experiments was, I believe, to determine whether a narrow-gauge railway, constructed on the principle of that at Aldershot, would fulfil certain conditions considered to be necessary for a railway especially adapted for war purposes, in order that the Committee might be able to judge from information obtained from actual experiment under what circumstances they could recommend the use of such a railway for the military transport service in time of war. As stated in the correspondence between the Royal Engineers Committee and myself, the conditions above named were as follows: 1st. That a railway, made upon the designs I had submitted to the Committee, should be proved to be capable of being constructed (the materials being prepared beforehand) with greater rapidity than an ordinary railway. The rate of construction, assumed to be possible with this improved system of narrow-gauge railway, was one mile of railway per day, over such a country as that of the experimental line at Aldershot, with the labour of 500 men; the greatest length of railway, hitherto made for war purposes, having been one mile per day, over an easy country, by the labour of 5,000 to 6,000 men...2nd. The other condition was, that the railway should be capable of carrying the quantity and description of ammunition, commissariat stores, &c., required for the service of an army in the field. This condition being defined as follows - viz., that a locomotive engine of 6 tons weight should draw a load of 30 tons gross weight up a gradient of 1 in 50, on a railway of 18 inches gauge, and travel at an average speed of from 10 to 20 miles an hour, according to the weight of the train and the gradients on the line...Also, that the wagons should be able to carry 3 tons each, and two wagons should carry one 7 ton siege gun. The capabilities of the railways constructed at Aldershot, for fulfilling these last-named requirements were put to severe and exhaustive tests during the trials made at intervals over a period of twelve months...The wagons were loaded with 3 tons each of shot and shell, casks of provisions, and with bulky articles such as tents and hay.

"The locomotive engine, although only 4.1/2 tons weight, took loads of 30 tons up a gradient of 1 in 50, and round sharp curves, and travelled...at average speeds of from 10 to 20 miles per hour, and at a maximum speed of 30 miles an hour. On no occasion did either the engine or any of the wagons leave the rails, the running of the trains was free from oscillation, and the strength of the railway was proved to be amply sufficient for carrying more powerful engines and heavier trains...I conclude, therefore, the results of the trials proved that the conditions...have been satisfactorily fulfilled; and...that (such) a narrow-gauge railway...is capable of effecting the transport of 1,000 tons of military stores per day, being, I am informed, a sufficient supply for an army of 100,000 men in the field.

"The experiments, made...with a view to show with what rapidity this system of railway could be constructed by military labour in time of war, were of a more limited character than those above referred to, but...were equally conclusive; and the result indicated that a greater length than one mile of railway could be made by 500 men in one day, and, consequently, that with this system 10 miles of field railway could be made for one mile of the ordinary form. I have every reason to believe the Committee will be satisfied that the facts, as I have stated them, are correct, that all the conditions...have been fulfilled by the results of the experiments, and that there are circumstances, as they observe in their report on the trials made at Parkhouse in 1871, under which such a railway for war purposes would be invaluable. I may add that, since the date of the Aldershot experiments, important improvements have been made in these light narrow-gauge railways, by which the power of the engines has been so much increased as to enable them to ascend gradients of 1 in 20, and to pass round curves of small radius. The structure has also been rendered more portable, and better adapted for military purposes. It is my conviction that, with a force of 2,000 or 2,500 men, perfectly efficient field railways on this principle can be constructed over a moderately undulating country (similar to that at Aldershot, or to the line made in the Franco-German War for 22 miles from Remuilly to Pont a Mousson) at the rate of 5 miles of railway per day, and that this rate of progress can be maintained for long distances.

"I understand, however, that before recommending the adoption of this system of narrow-gauge railways for the military transport service in time of war, the Committee now deem it necessary to see it in such general use in this country that a supply of rolling stock might, whenever required, be obtained from existing railways. This is a new condition - one rather of a financial than of an engineering character - which formed no part of the original programme of the experiments, and for compliance with which I cannot be considered responsible...Under these circumstances, and in order that I may not be prejudiced by any misconstruction which might be put on the views of the Committee, but on the contrary be able to derive any advantage to which I may be entitled from the results of the trials, I shall feel obliged if you will allow me to be furnished with a copy of the report of the Royal Engineers Committee, or a statement from them or from the War Department, containing a detailed account of the trials. And I hope it will be admitted that there is no reason why it should not be to the effect that, in an engineering point of view, the result of the experiments made on the narrow-gauge railway at Aldershot has been satisfactory and successful.

I have the honour to remain,
Sir,
Your most obedient servant,
JOHN B. FELL, C.E."

This letter was forwarded to the Committee who made the following observations upon it. Firstly, they saw no objection to Fell being furnished with a copy of their report. Secondly, they considered that while "the rate of one mile per day claimed by Mr Fell, appeared to be borne out from the work on one gang, it must be remembered that even with the eight gangs required for a mile*, very great additional difficulty would be experienced in bringing up and sorting the stores, and the total rate attainable on service cannot...be estimated by simply multiplying the number of gangs. Also...in countries without existing roads and railways, the means of bringing up the materials to the various points where the different gangs would begin work would not exist; and the rate per day mentioned by Mr Fell...(would) be quite impracticable on service". They also felt that Fell, "in his later patents having abandoned the use of side wheels on a narrow gauge, and adopted an ordinary gauge on trestles, in which the Committee fail to see any novelty, they did not consider that any special merit remains in his system". This statement is, as has been shown above, a distortion of the truth. Thirdly, the Committee, whilst admitting that Fell's line was capable of carrying the goods and passengers required of it, pointed out that any other kind of railway could do likewise; which is obvious.

Finally, the Committee observed that, "in the original report of the Sub-Committee...it was proposed to carry a load of 10 wagons up a slope of 1 in 12, while the line as constructed had a slope of only 1 in 50, up which a load of 25 tons, or 5 tons less than the weight of 10 empty wagons, was taken; and that the expected advantage of the side gripping wheels was not obtained, the side wheels though reinstating the stability of the train which was endangered by the reduction of the gauge, causing actually a diminution of the tractive power of the engine, instead of being an addition to it". Both of these statement are untrue. The weight of an empty wagon was 1.1/2 tons and 10 empty wagons would thus weigh 15 tons. The locomotive thus pulled 10 tons more than was required of it, albeit up an easier gradient. When, in 1870, the Committee requested a drawing, specification and cost of a locomotive from Fell, they specified a gradient of 1 in 50. A gradient of 1 in 12 is excessive for a railway relying only on the weight of the locomotive on the rails to provide traction and it has to be assumed that Fell had in mind the use of the guide wheels for traction, as in his centre rail system, when he made this claim. His centre rail line over Mont Cenis had gradients as steep as 1 in 10, the Rimutaka Incline in New Zealand (built by Fell in 1875) had a maximum gradient of 1 in 13 (an average of 1 in 15 for 2.1/2 miles) and his son's 1895 line to the summit of Snaefell, in the Isle of Man, had a gradient of 1 in 12 (this for 85% of its 4.66 miles) although in this case the centre rail was used only for braking. Fell had never specifically undertaken to use the guide wheels for additional traction at Aldershot (although his patents allowed for it) and neither had the Committee ever requested him to do so. Also, the Committee themselves had, as early as their visit to the Parkhouse line, remarked on the fact that the guide wheels only touched their rails at corners and then only slightly. This fact was further remarked upon during the first set of experiments at Aldershot.

Nevertheless, whatever the arguments as to the facts of the Aldershot experiments, the principle fact was that the army had turned its face firmly against Fell's proposals. It appears that the Aldershot Railway was retained for a time, as a means of instructing the troops on the operation of military railways, but the date of its eventual demise is not known. The Parkhouse Mineral Railway was replaced by a standard gauge branch in 1873 and was equipped, it is worth noting, with a Manning, Wardle locomotive (MW 450 of 1873 - YARLSIDE No 1). The proposals for guide rail lines in Fifeshire and between Lausanne and Lake Geneva do not appear to have borne fruit. Thus, Fell's proposals for guide rail lines died and passed into obscurity. His non-guide rail system, as represented by the Torrington and Marland Railway, fared somewhat better; some of his viaducts remaining until the 1920s. The patents for this system (and probably also for the guide rail system) were said by Fell (in April 1875) to belong to the 'Patent Narrow Gauge Co Ltd' which charged royalties at £100 per mile and £100 per locomotive; but the company never actually existed. However, neither of these systems had anything like the success he had hoped for. It was his original centre rail system which brought him the greatest acclaim and it was to the further improvement of that system that his final patent of 1895 was devoted. A patent number was also allocated to his name in 1892 for "Locomotive engines and permanent way" but, as the patent was never taken out, we have no way of knowing what it related to. The Rimutaka Incline was not replaced by a tunnel (5 miles long) until 3 November 1955 and the Snaefell Mountain Railway functions to this day. John Barraclough Fell died at his home at Southport on 18 October 1902, in his eighty-eighth year.

*Fell actually specified eight gangs of 30 men plus one foreman per half mile.

"IT'S FAILURE WAS CERTAIN"

On Monday 20th May 1878, J.B. Fell attended a meeting at the United Service Institution where Mr John L. Haddan read a paper on his proposals and patents for 'Pioneer' railways. These proposals were for light weight, prefabricated, steam powered monorails with guide wheels, of a type very similar to Fell's monorail proposals of 1868; as will be seen from the illustration. The details of the 'Pioneer' need not be gone into here except to stress that, whereas Fell virtually abandoned the monorail principle in favour of two bearing rails (the gauge of which depended on the situation) Haddan clung tenaciously to it. Haddan also eschewed Fell's high trestles, opting instead for low single posts combined with very steep gradients. Haddan's proposed lines were, like Fell's, intended (among other things) for the rapid construction of military supply railways.

In the course of his lecture, Haddan made scathing comments on Fell's railway at Aldershot, stating that..."its failure was certain, for on such a structure a gravity engine would have to be four times as heavy to do the same work as on an ordinary railway; because, from the fact of cuttings not being used to compensate the banks in forming grades, inclines of say twice the steepness would be required to grade the same line of country. In lieu of a 10 foot bank, compensating a 10 foot cutting; a 20 foot viaduct is required to obtain the same grade: or, if a 10 foot viaduct were substituted, grades would have to be so steep that the engine would have to weigh fourfold (see diagrams). Thus at Aldershot on easy ground, it was necessary to use 20 foot trestles to secure a grade of 1 in 50, and a paltry gross load of only 22 tons, or say 14 tons net. The weight per axle was the same as the Pioneer. Now such lofty posts are not economical, since a 5 foot post will support about four times the amount which a 20 foot post would do; consequently their habitual use is not practical. These trestles have also the additional inconvenience in a ready-made railway, of requiring a proportionately greater stock of type trestles of various heights, whose component parts all differ both in size, weight, and angle, and, therefore, cannot be used in common.

Haddan's 'Pioneer' railway.   *(Collection Peter Holmes)*

"On this system there could be no universal standard trestle applicable, or even readily convertible, to any country, even an easy one; and most elaborate levels, both longitudinal and transverse (as in setting out side widths on a railway) would have to be performed on the proposed site of each trestle, and guys and other tackle used for the erection of all but the smallest sizes. On curves, more especially if a 3ft 6in gauge were used, as suggested by Mr Fell, not a piece would fit, as the right and left beams and rails are either longer or shorter, especially on a road where the curves throughout had a tendency, say more right than left...All post and rail railways claim the advantage of abolishing earthworks, but the Aldershot railway employs cuttings, the earth from which is not utilized at all..."

At the conclusion of the lecture, comments were invited from the audience, and the comments of J.B. Fell serve to neatly summarise his experimental work with narrow gauge railways. "Mr Haddan has made some remarks on an experimental line that I carried out at Aldershot, to which I should like to reply; but, before doing so, I wish to say I agree with Mr Haddan...that, for military purposes, earthworks ought to be superseded by a structure of some kind - it may be of wood, or of iron - it may be one rail, two rails, or three rails - but it must be structure of some kind. Earthworks cannot be executed, that is, if they exceed four or six feet in height or depth, within the time required for military purposes, and, when executed, they would be so liable to get out of order; their subsidence would be so frequent, from rains and other causes, that a railway made with earthworks, exceeding six feet in depth, would be for a long time practically useless; indeed, the railways constructed during the Franco-German War round Metz, with the labour of 4,000 men, in about a month, was worked for about thirty days only, and during that time was found to be almost useless. The question under consideration is that, if a railway has to be made with great rapidity, and required to be used immediately it is made, what kind of structure is best for the purpose?

Mr Haddan has attempted to demonstrate that a single rail is best.

"Now, I have come to the conclusion, from seven years' experience, that a structure with a single rail is the worst that can be used. I have tried both, and I have found two rails answer very much better than one rail. I began by making experiments in the north of England with a single rail railway. Captain (now Sir Henry) Tyler did me the favour to look at it, and also to look at a very narrow gauge railway erected near Barrow-in-Furness, with an 8 inch gauge, the 8 inch gauge railway worked very much better than a single rail. When I made proposals to the War Office to put up an experimental line at Aldershot, I increased the 8 inch gauge to 18, and the 18 inch gauge worked better than the 8. I have now come to the conclusion that it would be better to have, at least, a 2 feet 6 inch or 3 feet gauge, and I believe a 3 feet gauge railway will work better than an 18 inch gauge, and better than a single rail. One considerable objection to a single rail, or to any very narrow gauge, brought to my notice by the Royal Engineers Committee, was that it would require a special kind of rolling stock. You have all your rolling stock to make when required for use, unless it is kept in store, and no Government likes to go to the expense of keeping many miles of a particular kind of railway in store for, it may be, use within five or ten years, and the War Department made this objection to the 18 inch gauge, and that was one reason why, in the plans which I afterwards prepared, I proposed to use a 3 feet gauge. Another reason is this, that by using a 3 feet gauge you may altogether dispense with the guide wheels. If you have guide wheels when the line is on the surface, you must necessarily raise your structure a considerable height above the ground, being so much labour thrown away, and so much carpentry work to keep in order, which is entirely unnecessary.

"Mr Haddan has claimed for his particular form of one rail railway great economy in construction. Now, the structure has to be made of sufficient strength to carry the weight of the engine and wagons, and whether you put the whole of that strength into one or two posts I cannot see that it affects the supporting power; but if you put it into two posts, and connect those posts together, while you have the same bearing power, you have very considerable lateral strength, which you do not get when the vertical support is all put into one centre post, without any lateral struts to steady it. Therefore, at Aldershot, I adopted a form of this kind: first of all, there was the centre post and then two lateral posts; afterwards, I dispensed with the lateral posts, and had the two outside posts only on a very light post in the middle, merely to bind the whole structure together. I think it would be a very considerable advantage, in any military railway where a structure is used, to be able to use it in connection with an ordinary surface line. I think when the country permits of a line being laid on the surface with a gauge of 3 feet, or a metre, which will be sufficient for this purpose, the ordinary cross-sleeper form of permanent way is the very best that can be used, and has great advantages to the single rail system proposed by Mr Haddan. A railway of this kind, or of the kind we had at Aldershot, forms a barrier

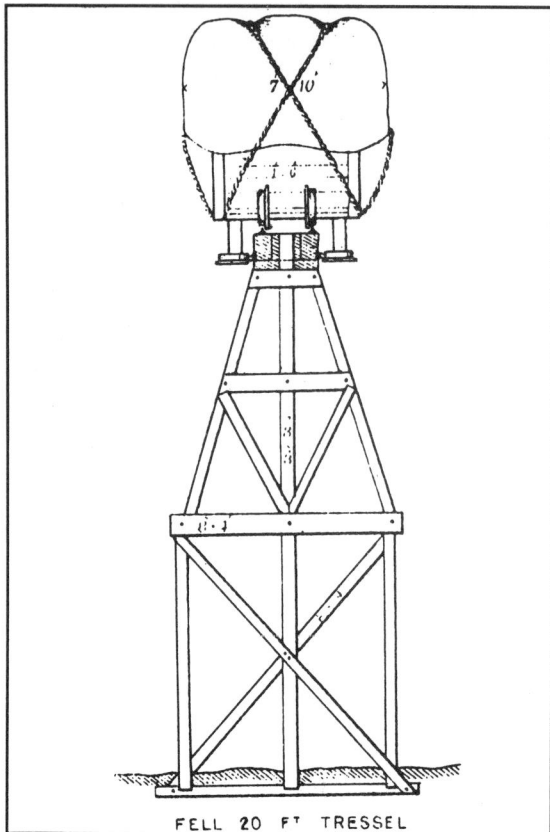

FELL 20 FT TRESSEL

movable bridge over the railway, or you must make a portion of the railway to open...You may want level crossings very frequently, in some countries. At Aldershot, we found considerable inconvenience from this cause. You cannot use the ordinary points and crossings, which is a great disadvantage. Therefore, if you can use the ordinary surface line along with the structure, you gain the advantage of the structure for going over uneven ground, and the advantage, also, of being able to use the simplest and best form of railway where no structure is required. Mr Haddan observed that, at Aldershot, we put in a viaduct of unnecessary height. As he has shown, by that diagram, there is a viaduct, to cross a valley, of 25 feet in height. That is true, but Mr Haddan was not quite aware of the circumstances under which that line was made. It was purely as an experimental line, and not as selecting the best line of country, and that viaduct was put in on purpose that we might have a viaduct, and that we might find out what would be the action of a train running at a high speed and with a load 25 feet above the level of the ground. It was put in exactly for that, and no other purpose.

"What I should propose at the present time would be, in such a case, to make a slight cutting. He has shown a 10 feet cutting and a 10 feet embankment. That, of course, is an exaggerated section. You would not find a country like it. There would be longer cuttings and longer embankments than those. Instead of filling up the whole 20 feet, I should propose making a cutting of

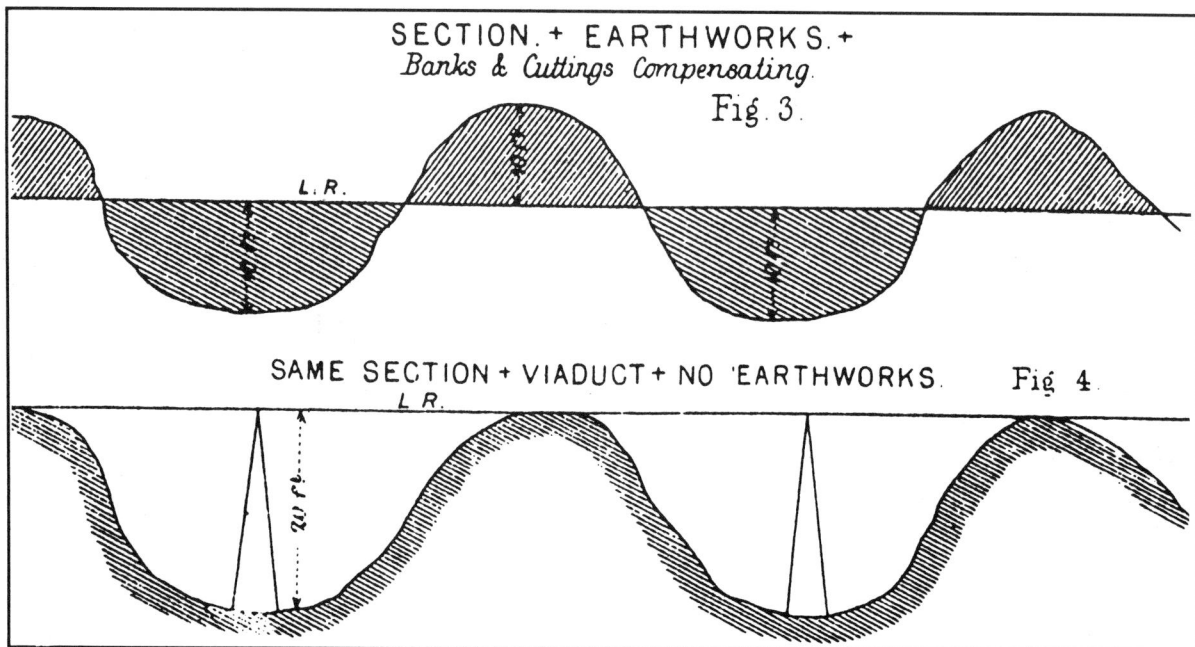

SECTION. + EARTHWORKS. +
Banks & Cuttings Compensating.
Fig. 3.

L.R.

SAME SECTION + VIADUCT + NO EARTHWORKS.   Fig 4.
L.R.

Diagrams from Mr Haddan's Paper to the United Service Institution

34

2, 3, or 5 feet, and fill up the rest with a structure. In that way you might execute just as much earthworks, and use just as much structure, as circumstances rendered desirable. Then, with regard to rapidity of execution, I do not know whether Mr Haddan has made experiments, for any length of time, with that form of structure, in order to prove what length could be put up, with a certain number of men in a certain time, but at Aldershot we worked away from March to June, 1873, in order to ascertain, for a structure of that kind, what number of men would be required to execute a mile in a day. The programme agreed upon was that we should be able to make one mile a day with 500 men over similar country to that at Aldershot, and using military labour alone; a few sappers were used, but the rest were men of the line. One half of the railway was taken down and re-erected. Each set of men had about a week's practice, and when the Royal Engineers Committee came down to see the experiment, we were working at the rate of two miles a day with 500 men, so that we performed double the amount of work required by the programme. I think Mr Haddan used the word 'failure' in connection with the railway at Aldershot. I have with me a copy of the Royal Engineers Committee's report, given me by the Secretary of State for War, in which he does not call it a failure, but in which he certifies that the whole of the programme, both as regards the loads to be carried, duty to be performed by the engine, as regards speed and so on, and also as regards the power of constructing the railway with great rapidity, has been satisfactorily fulfilled, and, therefore, I think it would be doing me an injustice if it were to go abroad to this meeting and the public that the work I undertook to do at Aldershot was a failure. I can show any gentleman, who chooses to take the trouble to look at it, the report in which it is stated that, instead of it being a failure, all the conditions of the programme were satisfactorily fulfilled...I entirely agree with Mr Haddan in this one thing, that earthworks must be dispensed with, but I certainly think a gauge of some kind, let it be 18 inches, 2 feet, or 3 feet, is very much better than a railway without any gauge at all...It has been said the system of railway I proposed to the War Department is very expensive. The War Department has received a tender from very responsible contractors to construct the railway at £2,500 a mile, which is a very moderate price."

SOURCES:

Furness Folk and Facts by William White (Kendal - Titus Wilson + Son, 1930)
Minutes of Proceedings of the Institution of Civil Engineers (Vol.151, 1903)
The Barrow Herald, January and November 1870
Engineering, 23 September 1870, 8 December 1871, 5 July 1872, 15 November 1872, 10 August 1877
        and 28 December 1894
The Engineer, 17 November 1871, 1 November 1872, 15 November 1872 and 13 December 1872
Extracts from the "Proceedings of the Royal Engineers Committee, 1870 - 1875"

The patents of John Barraclough Fell in The Patent Office, London; which are as follows:

Patent number		Date	Description
	227	26 Jan 1863	Working railway engines and carriages on steep inclines. (a)
	3182	16 Dec 1863	Railway engines and carriages, etc. (a)
	2174	24 Aug 1866	Locomotive engines and carriages. (a)
	766	5 Mar 1868	Locomotive engines, carriages, etc. (b)
	899	24 Mar 1869	Locomotive engines, railways, etc. (a)
	1	2 Jan 1871	Locomotive engines. (c)
	1246	9 May 1871	Railways. (c)
	1014	19 Mar 1873	Light railways. (With G.N. Fell) (d)
	1638	26 Apr 1879	Light railways and locomotive engines. (d)
	1249	24 Mar 1880	Railways. (d)
	3579	28 Jul 1882	Locomotive engines. (d)
	6718	7 Apr 1892	Locomotive engines and permanent way. (e)
	762	12 Jan 1895	Improvements in engines for traction. (a)

(a)   The centre rail system
(b)   The 'monorail patent'
(c)   Elevated narrow gauge railways with guide rails
(d)   Elevated narrow gauge railways without guide rails
(e)   Patent not taken out

The Locomotive, 15 June 1939
The Railway Magazine, January 1961
The Pentewan Railway by M.J.T. Lewis (Twelveheads Press, 1981 - first
        published by D.B. Barton, Truro, 1960)
North Devon Clay by M.J. Messenger (Twelveheads Press, 1982)
Minimum Gauge Railways by Sir Arthur Percival Heywood (Third Edition of
        1898 - reprinted by Turntable Publications, Sheffield, 1974)
Isle of Man Tramways by F.K. Pearson (David and Charles, Newton Abbott, 1970)
A Hunslet Hundred by L.T.C. Rolt (David and Charles/MacDonald, 1964)
The Pioneer or Steam Caravan by J.L. Haddan (London, 1878)

Thanks must also go to the Hunslet Engine Co of Leeds who supplied information and copies of the original drawings of the locomotives built by Manning, Wardle and Co.

Useful information on the Parkhouse mines and reference to the Parkhouse Mineral Railway and J.L. Haddan came from Peter Holmes.

For an analysis of the developing awareness of the value of railways in European warfare at this period see *The Franco-Prussian War* by Michael Howard (Methuen, 1981) pages 2 to 4.

I would like to thank Michael J Messenger and Dr M.J.T. Lewis for supplying photographs and Jane Townsend for producing an excellent portrait of J.B. Fell from a very poor photographic original.

Finally, my thanks to Angie, to whom this work is dedicated.

E.A. Wade, July 1986